# FACING ANGER

## HOW TO TURN LIFE'S MOST **TROUBLESOME EMOTION** INTO A PERSONAL ASSET

## Norman Rohrer
and
## S. Philip Sutherland

**AUGSBURG** Publishing House • Minneapolis

FACING ANGER

MANUFACTURED IN THE UNITED STATES OF AMERICA

# Contents

A Perspective      5

**Understanding Anger**
1    All Us Angry People      8
2    Myths about Anger      18
3    A Response, Not a Reflex      32

**Sources of Anger**
4    The Desire to Feel Powerful      44
5    The Desire to Feel Self-Sufficient      56
6    The Desire to Feel Important      66
7    The Desire to Be Perfect      77

**Dealing with Anger**
8    How to Handle Anger in Others      92
9    How to Handle Anger in Yourself      114

Suggested Reading      128

# A Perspective

No one can live a rich and full life without anger. Like love, it is part of the structure of the soul.

Anger has other functions than to smash, hurt, spoil, and destroy. It can establish values, correct injustice, halt outrageous fortune, and promote growth. A person without anger cares about little, cannot love, and is not likely to experience supreme joy.

Who could write a great symphony without anger at mediocre scores? What would the imprecatory psalms be without sanctified anger?

*Facing Anger* is not a how-to book for getting rid of this perturbation, but a blueprint for synthesizing anger—breaking it up into manageable parts and using them constructively—and turning it into an asset. *Facing Anger* is for people who have reason to think that suppressed anger might be spoiling their lives, interrupting warm human relationships, and keeping them from enjoying a happy, satisfying, fulfilling life.

The river of destructive anger is fed by four sources:

- a lack of the feeling of power over people and circumstances;

- a lack of the feeling of self-sufficiency;

- a diminished feeling of importance; and

- frustration in the face of unachievable perfection.

Jesus Christ tamed destructive anger with the "whip" of a tender plant, a broken reed, a root out of dry ground. When those he came to save refused to hear him, when he had no place to lay his head, when he was considered less to be desired than a murderer, and when the perfect kingdom he came to establish was rejected, he accepted humiliation and "reviled not again."

Everyone has a choice when faced with the struggle for power, self-sufficiency, importance, and perfection. We can choose either to become angry and try to intimidate in order to stay on top or, like Jesus, we can choose to be humble, meek, and poor in spirit, not returning evil for evil.

Shouldering Jesus' yoke is not always easy, but it is the secret of a happy life. All who synthesize their anger will experience blessed release: "God accepts me just as I am." And others will too, when we stop trying to get the upper hand.

Be angry and sin not.

# UNDERSTANDING ANGER

# One

## All Us Angry People

Anger is a human being's first emotion, and it is often the last. Thomas Fuller the divine called anger "part of the sinew of the soul." It can be nursed and made savage or synthesized and turned into an asset. It can keep people alive or hasten their death. Anger has started every war and anger has ended every war.

Babies express anger by crying, but later they use it to stand alone in a demanding world. Children exhibit anger with teasing, sarcasm, and practical jokes; in adults it surfaces as prejudice, gossip, domination, suicide, and rape. It also is a component of passive human experience revealed as depression, guilt, withdrawal, the "super-sweet" personality, pouting, silence, and moodiness. It can be part of tickling, competing, arguing, love-making, shooting, killing, and destroying.

### What is anger?

Anger is an emotion. It arises when a wish or a desire is not fulfilled. When a desire is not fulfilled, we feel an urge to change that situation or to destroy it. Anger, then, is an urge to attack somebody or some thing for the purpose of altering or destroying it. Or, anger can be deflected away from the primary object of anger and displaced onto a substitute object. This happens when the primary object of anger is too powerful or too necessary in our lives to risk attacking it.

Anything that prevents us from gaining what we want is called a frustration. We say our goals or desires are frustrated when they cannot be obtained. Frustration is the event, and the emotional response to frustration is what we call anger. Technically the expression "I feel frustrated" is inaccurate. We can *be* frustrated, but the emotion we usually feel when frustrated is anger or hostility.

## Who is angry?

Can you tell when a person is angry? Test yourself in this visit to the home of J. Courtney Bower and his wife, Betty Sue. As we look in on this average American couple of suburbia we find Mrs. Bower seated in the living room of her home with a cluster of friends. They are planning a bazaar.

Betty Sue, 30 pounds overweight, excuses herself and trips to the door as her burly husband storms in from a day on the road. She notices a scratch on his hand and kisses it dramatically.

"Oh, you poor dear!" she exclaims. "What happened?"

"Forget it—just a scratch," Courtney booms as he tosses his briefcase on the sofa.

Betty Sue runs to get a Band-Aid and his slippers. She shows him where the newspaper is, then hurries into the living room to rejoin her guests. Before they leave she has volunteered to collect the tickets and to provide the main dish for the meal.

The woman is dressed in dainty frills; her house is immaculate; a full-course dinner is prepared for her husband and children; they will eat precisely on time. Women whisper: "Betty Sue—I don't know how she does it!"

She keeps hidden a drawer full of overdue bills and says nothing about a gnawing pain in her stomach.

Courtney slams his sales catalog against the hall closet door. "Why do I put up with this job?" he growls. "The boss promised 30 percent on the Bellmeade project. What do I get? More promises."

He spots his son's soccer ball in the hallway and begins kicking it against the baseboard: *rat-a-tat-a-tat*. "Oh, well," he sighs, peeling off his shoes, "it's a good company anyhow."

He changes into his overalls and goes out to finish painting the house.

Which person is angry?

Both, but sweet little Betty Sue keeps a tight lid on hers while her husband turns his anger into constructive work. He has learned to synthesize his anger and make it work *for* him instead of *against* him.


## Sources of anger

From birth to death, people experience frustration and the resulting emotion: anger. Whenever we protest because things are not as we want them to be, whenever we try to change, destroy, or attack people, places, or things, we are experiencing anger.

Some people find it easy to recognize their urge to

10

attack; many others find it extremely difficult to admit to such feelings. They use a variety of tricks and mechanisms to deny that they are actually angry.

In the stories that follow you will see how a person can be angry and not feel it, how another can feel it and not express it, how still another can both feel it and express it, and finally, how a person can be angry but neither feel it nor express it. You will see how people use anger for power, for self-sufficiency, for importance, and for perfection.


*Power*

A disheveled chap named Paul was a perfect example of a person who substituted anger for feelings of weakness. He entered the clinic one day with a pistol in his coat pocket. Obviously he was agitated. He sat rigid on the edge of the couch rather than lying down and talking in a relaxed manner. His hands pushed back and forth across his knees.

"What would you do if I brought a gun in here and threatened to shoot you?" he asked the therapist. Paul's eyes brightened mischievously at the prospect of emptying a gun into somebody's head.

"What would you do if I held a gun to your head?"

"How would you hope I would react?"

"I would want you to crawl and squirm and beg for mercy."

"How would that make you feel?"

"Then *I* would be in charge! I would be powerful, I would dominate the world, I could get revenge. . . ."

With his gun, Paul was king! He could rule with great power; he could intimidate. When the therapist suggested that Paul's true feeling was weakness and that he needed a gun to restore power, he denied it.

"That's not true! It's just more convenient, that's all."

The feeling of rage supported by his gun was indeed the exact opposite of what Paul felt on a deeper level. His weapon offered power; his heart only offered despised weakness and impotence.

The feeling of weakness grows out of people's deep desires. As the feeling of weakness grows, angry persons fear that those they depend upon might reject them or turn on them in anger. So, to avoid feelings of weakness, they call on anger to give them a sense of strength. They want desperately to enjoy feelings of competence, strength, and security through another person without having to be active themselves. At the same time they are irritated because they are so easily influenced by the strong persons whom they admire. They can't resist the wishes of other people and therefore are easily dominated. Result? Feelings that they are frivolous, insignificant, vile, base, ignoble, and downright worthless. Who can tolerate that?

## Self-sufficiency

Not everyone who exhibits anger desires to gain power over others. Some people react to a situation with anger in order to restore a sense of self-sufficiency.

"I hate you!" fumed the petite, 102-pound client named Helen. Her hands quivered as though she would like nothing better than to strangle her therapist. "Stay away from me! I don't need you. I don't need *anybody!*"

As an infant and young child Helen had felt helpless

and needy, but her mother could not accept those feelings in her little daughter. When Helen's mother hugged and cuddled her something would snap, and the mother would jump up and brush Helen aside. "You're a nuisance!" she would cry. "I'm sorry you were ever born!" After saying that, the mother would stomp out of the room—sometimes out of the house.

Helen grew to maturity with her emotional guard up. It became clear to her early on that if she *wanted* to be with people this desire would drive them away. Therefore, when strong impulses to enjoy human relationships would come upon her, she would resist them with rage. Helen is intelligent, and her rational mind is aware of the illogical way she feels. However, strong feelings persist nevertheless. Like millions of people, Helen, at a deep level, fears her desires and needs. When they come upon her she retreats into a safe substitute—anger.


*Importance*

Paul—angry for power; Helen—angry for self-sufficiency. Next, an example of anger to keep from feeling unimportant.

"I get so mad when I'm driving I could . . ."

"Why?" asked Sherry's therapist.

"Because there are stupid drivers out there."

"Why do 'stupid drivers' bother you?"

"Because they're always in my way."

"They have a right to be there too. Why does it bother you that they are on the road?"

Sherry believed she deserved special treatment in every area of life—including the right-of-way on public roads. In childhood she had been the center of attention among doting parents and two brothers. On a deep level Sherry assumed the whole world should treat her as special as her family did.

"It sounds silly," Sherry admitted, but she would rather feel angry than face the humiliating truth that she had no more rights than the next person.


### Perfection

Paul used anger to be powerful; Helen used anger to be self-sufficient; Sherry used anger to be important; and now another phenomenon: the use of anger to hold on to the illusion of perfection.

Jim couldn't bring himself to admit that he had actually committed a foul against another basketball player. He kicked the ball in a fit of rage.

The intense young man had played basketball since he was in the seventh grade. In his mind his game was perfect. He had never committed a foul in his life. This drive for perfection had propelled Jim toward good grades and athletic stardom, but he remained angry nearly all the time while vehemently blaming others for his mistakes.

What will happen to him? If Jim is like most perfectionists, he will either relax and give up the fantasy or else he will drive harder to grasp the illusion. In this posture he will become an excellent candidate for involvement in some social activist crusade, lashing out at the society which he sees as too demanding. Like millions of other people, Jim would rather remain angry and blame others for his mistakes than face any inadequacy in himself.

## How to identify anger

To determine whether or not people are angry, first observe their "body language." If they cross their legs, fold their arms across their chests, intertwine fingers, bounce their feet, push fingers and thumbs together, sit forward in the chair, or frown, you have some clues about what is going on inside. The body pays heavy dues for anger. The effects can be tension in the upper back and lower neck areas, headaches, colitis, ulcers, hypertension, rashes, and chronic fatigue.

Second, ask a person you think might be angry, "What would your hands do if they could do whatever they wanted?" (This removes responsibility for feelings and loosens inhibitions.) The angry person might respond with answers like: "My hands would tear you apart; I'd like to choke somebody; I'd throw this _____ into the sea; I'd like to scratch . . . slug . . . claw. . . ."

Third, observe actions. Angry people swear, spit, argue, walk away abruptly, or give others the silent treatment. Such behavior is not always the direct result of anger, but it often is.


## Why are people angry?

Anger is not an automatic reflex that involuntarily erupts following a provocation. Angry people *choose* it to prevent a loss of self-esteem. It's a hedge against humiliation.

Haven't you seen people throw up a smoke screen of anger to spare themselves the full impact of some real or imagined loss?

Observe:

15

- "You cheated!" screamed Mary as Barbara picked up the final jack and won the game. Mary's anger was cleverly designed to prevent her humiliation.

- "Psssst. Joan is having an affair, but don't tell anybody," Betty whispered to her two friends. This bit of gossip put her on top of her "enemy."

- "I'll show *her*," muttered John as he tore up the note from his ex-fiance. He grabbed the phone and called the loosest girl on campus for a date. It was his way of raising a shield against his bitter defeat.

Most people need their anger to support the fantasy that they are indeed as powerful, self-sufficient, important, and perfect as they wish they were. Their anger quotient is measured by their true feelings beneath the facade. Often those true feelings are kept tightly locked.

To this question, "What would you feel if you weren't angry?" the response is usually superficial: "Oh, I'd feel peaceful and calm." But when people are encouraged to pursue their true feelings they discover this to be untrue. In reality, their anger is keeping them from feeling not peace and tranquility but other "intolerable" emotions such as depression and a loss of the coveted "good guy" position, the image of competence, or the illusion of greatness.

### Summary

Anger is an emotion—specifically an urge to attack. The urge arises when a desire is not fulfilled. The desires that are not being fulfilled can usually be classified under one of the following four categories: The desire for power, the desire for self-sufficiency, the desire for importance, the desire for perfection.

People can be angry and not feel it, feel it and not express it, and both feel it *and* express it. Anger is not an automatic reflex. Anger is a *chosen* emotion whose purpose is to avoid some form of humiliation. No one can be made angry against his will.

# Two

# Myths about Anger

Anger can be quite a bothersome emotion. One hardly thinks of anger without attaching to it all kinds of unpleasant consequences.

Trouble with anger begins in earliest childhood. When children become angry they quickly learn that parents and friends tend to leave them alone. They then feel abandoned and sad. As children we are warned that acting angrily is bad and punishable. Feeling angry and acting angrily are considered bad, naughty, sinful. So we avoid being angry in order to be admired. Nobody wants to be close to an angry person. Angry people can make it tough on others, often causing retaliation and *always* causing apprehension.

"Watch out! He's mad!"

All these fears have caused people to deny they are angry. In the process, many myths about anger have grown up. To understand anger completely, we need to shatter those myths.

## Myth 1: Anger is merely an action

It is natural to think of anger only as an emotion connected to action—smashing, hurting, striking out with temper. Angry people go right along with the game. They say things like "I'm not angry, I'm just teasing," or "Sure, I'll forgive you, but don't expect me to forget what you did!"

People who expect anger to always be visible will say things like: "She doesn't seem angry," or "I can't understand why he did that; he seemed like such a nice person."

More anger by far is felt than "telt." People who are angry do not always express their anger. Indeed, as we showed earlier, not everyone who is angry is even aware of their anger. This is illustrated in the following situations.

Four persons were cheated at the cash register of a supermarket. The first gave the cashier a tongue lashing, the second mumbled his displeasure under his breath, the third ignored the fact that it happened, the fourth justified the cashier's action by explaining: "She was just too busy. . . ."

The first two responses are examples of angry *behavior;* the third and fourth responses are examples of angry *feelings.* The first two indicate that the angry person did something about the cheating; the third and fourth had a strong momentary angry impulse but got rid of it by denying and justifying the cheating. Quite possibly the third and fourth persons were not even aware of their anger. They would probably even deny that they were angry, having submerged the feeling for so many years.

People who defend someone who wronged them

19

reveal that they have already attacked them subconsciously. Defensive action makes no sense unless there has been an attack. The defense is an attempt to quickly get rid of the urge to attack. Both the attack and the defense of the cashier have taken place inside the person's head.

## Myth 2: All angry people know they're angry

John, a husky bricklayer, sat on the couch with his hand clenched, his knuckles white. He was angry although he would not admit it. He would not admit it because he wasn't actually aware of it. His "attack" was expressed in mild humor.

John stretched out on the couch.

"It appears that you are angry," his therapist noted.

The client shot back a vulgar directive without batting an eye. He emphasized it with a gesture. These actions proved that he was indeed an angry man, even though he refused to experience it. He had *behaved* angrily but he would not let himself *feel* his anger. This is common: a smile on the face, hands in the lap, and rage in the heart.

"Me, angry? Of course I'm not angry. I'm not angry, I tell you . . . *do you hear me? I'm NOT angry!*"

Others might remain completely placid and deny their anger, then turn right around and stick daggers into people with gossip, ridicule, and intimidation. Still others can argue, criticize, frustrate, or present a "syrupy-sweet" countenance.

Like John the bricklayer, prim little Patricia was able to sit on her anger for the sake of expedience. She was a proficient word processor but during a job interview she was intimidated by the interviewer. She took it sweetly, but afterward she told a friend, "I was so embarrassed I could have *killed* him."

"Did you tell him how you felt?" her friend asked.

"No, I wanted the job too badly."

John, the bricklayer, had expressed his anger but had not felt it; Patricia had felt her anger but did not express it. The next situation shows how a person can be angry and neither express it nor feel it.

Peter was a good child—quiet and cooperative. One day, for no apparent reason, he wrung his cat's neck. "I really didn't mean to kill my cat," he said. "I just loved it so much that I squeezed it to death." Peter could allow himself neither to experience anger nor to express it.

Same with a farmer boy 3000 miles away from Peter. His father called him "Sonny," and the boy was mild-mannered and calm. One day while Sonny was killing chickens in a poultry dressing shed his sister wandered by, stroking a kitty whose eyes were sore.

"Here," Sonny said, "I'll take care of your cat." He took the kitten with his left hand and laid it on his chopping block. With his cleaver he severed the cat's head from its body while his sister went crying to the house.

The innocent prank of a happy farm boy? Sonny had quit high school at the age of 14, unable to cope with his feelings of shyness. Now he was 19 without prospects for college. He was stuck on the farm and the outlook was bleak. Although his anger was not against the cat, the helpless feline was a handy victim. Afraid of his tenderness and also of his rage, Sonny killed the cat with hardly a second thought. He explained that he put the cat out of its misery. Perhaps he was wishing the same thing for himself.

21

## Myth 3: Anger is the same as aggression

Anger is an emotion—a desire to attack. Anger can be expressed and not felt (John the bricklayer and his vulgar directive), felt but not expressed (prim Patricia, the word processor), and neither felt nor expressed (mild Peter). Now we come to another step in the understanding of this universal emotion: anger versus aggression.

Angry behavior is often aggressive, but it is important to recognize that anger and aggression are not the same. Anger is an emotion which is the desire to attack; aggression is a motive which is the desire to assert oneself.

Most sentences beginning with "I" are aggressive sentences. "I love apple cobbler"—a statement of assertion about oneself. "I hate you"—a statement expressing both anger and aggression. "I want to go to church" —a statement of aggression. "I want to kill somebody"— a statement of both anger and aggression.

Aggression is an attempt to make one's presence and desires known. Our discussion of anger in this book will be limited to the desire to attack; it will not include aggression, which leads one merely to assert.

## Myth 4: Righteous indignation is not anger

Some people deny they are angry by convincing themselves they are only "righteously indignant." Now there's nothing wrong with righteous indignation. Anger *is* justified in some situations (e.g., Christ's cleansing of the temple). But just because there are justifiable reasons for anger does not change the nature of the emotion. The point is, anger is anger. Righteous indignation *is* anger.

If people are not convinced that their anger is justified, they may go to great lengths to identify their anger as righteous indignation. This suggests that they view all anger as bad, sinful, or pathological. This is not true. Normal, emotionally healthy people experience anger. People who try to deny their anger view themselves as good, moral, and exceptionally upright. Since anger damages this idealistic view of themselves, they deny what is going on inside rather than think of themselves as anything but pure, dependable, and exemplary.

Can there be unselfish or non-self-centered issues behind anger? Consider Jesus Christ. He was angry at people who were charging exorbitant interest rates and selling sacred objects in the temple unfairly, so he threw over the money tables. He wanted the people of Israel to be spiritually pure, to focus in on God, on important things, not on commercialism. He wanted poor people as well as the wealthy to experience spiritual celebration. These money-changers were charging outlandish rates for the sacrificial animals. Jesus' goal had to do with perfection not in himself but in other people (although Jesus also must have felt a loss of importance). It is obvious that he was identifying with God and that these people were not putting God first. Jehovah is a jealous God. He demands to be first because he deserves to be first.

In the Old Testament God is angry when people don't put him first, when people put him on a lower level than he is. God is more powerful, holy, and loving than anything created. If we trust him with less honor than he deserves he justifiably is angry. His goal is to have people respect him for who he is. After all, God is really God. He is not applying for the job.

If we humans become angry because we are not treated like God—important, powerful, self-sufficient, and perfect—this is unrealistic. If we are treated less importantly than we expect, what are we saying? We are implying that we are better and deserve more. How did Jesus react when slighted? He humbled himself and offered to serve. He never insisted on preferred treatment even though he deserved it. People owe us no special treatment, but we owe God everything.

The righteously indignant usually blame people around them for their anger. They consider others "morally calloused" or "too stubborn" or "unwilling to face the consequences of their actions." Often the righteously indignant say they are angry because of the way others are treating God, but just as often they are actually angry because of the way others are treating them.

For example, a pastor berated his congregation for not tithing. In reality he was angry at the loss of his own prestige as he admonished his people: "You're not giving God what you owe him." He was actually saying, "You're not giving *me* what you owe *me*. You're not making me the successful pastor I want to be." Few people are so perfect that their real concern is for God and not themselves or their business or their community or their country.

Imagine the loss of power and importance felt by the prophet Elijah in 1 Kings 18. As he interceded for the people of Israel he demanded that they choose between God and Baal. The people, however, did not answer him a word. He must have been angry, because he began to mock them and use sarcasm against the prophets of Baal, teasing them and thus revealing his anger.

How do you explain, then, that Elijah was a man of God doing God's assigned duties? Elijah handled his anger maturely. Rather than pout and condemn, he called the people to a situation which would force them to face the issues. Elijah's anger was synthesized by his good judgment, concern, and patience. The fire fell, the people faced the issue, God was glorified.

Now notice how an evangelist in a midwestern church acted in a similar situation. He had berated a congregation for not working harder to bring their friends to a two-week evangelistic meeting. Following a third disappointing night he appealed passionately for responders. When they did not appear he slammed his Bible shut and ended the meeting. He could not persuade the people to do what he wanted them to do, so he felt a great loss of power. If the evangelist had called his anger righteous indignation he would have been confusing the issue. He had spent much more time on the golf course that week than in calling in the homes of the people, and had prepared no new, fresh sermons for the pulpit. The evangelist should have asked: "Do I want glory for God or glory for myself? Would I be willing to serve as Jesus did when he was rejected? Am I missing an opportunity to be humble, sad, broken before the Lord?"

## Myth 5: Anger can be built up and stored

For many years psychologists and lay counselors thought anger could be accumulated until it had built up a head of steam that was too powerful for an individual to control. This is changing. A closer examination shows that anger can't be stockpiled or pressurized. It is not precisely accurate to say "If I get much more angry I'll explode!" or "That's the last straw! Now I'm *really* mad!"

Since anger can't be stockpiled or pressurized, what is going on in the head of an angry person? Such a person sees himself increasingly less powerful, important, self-sufficient, or perfect. Finally he "explodes" in anger in order to get back these attributes which he feels he has lost.

For example, someone pulls into my lane as I drive to work and slows me down. I'm miffed. As a result I miss the green light up ahead, and I'm already late for work. Now I'm angry. As I pull into the driveway behind my office I meet a huge truck which is blocking the narrow alley. I drive a block out of my way to the other entrance and I pick up a nail in the little-used passageway. All this time I'm feeling less and less powerful, less and less in control. So when I step inside the office I prepare to "explode" in anger to get back my sense of power, importance, self-sufficiency, and perfection.

But as I walk through the office door on that fateful morning my boss greets me with a pair of tickets to the Super Bowl and says, "Good news, you've been promoted! Come in here, we've got a celebration planned for you."

Suddenly all anger is gone. The bad circumstances en route to work are still remembered, but now I do not need to become angry in order to get on top and restore my sense of power. I have been recognized and made to feel important without exploding or spouting off in anger. It is not a release of anger that has been accomplished but a restored sense of power, importance, self-sufficiency, or perfection. Catharsis helps not because it reduces pressure but because it increases one's sense of worth through the strength which acting out of anger provides.

If people will deal with their loss, they need not become angry. Spouting off is, in the long run, anti-reality. "It's *your* fault!" is never an accurate charge.

People who use anger to gain power over other people are not *accumulating* anger, they are simply running out of ways to control other people. Anger is their last resort and they "explode," thinking they can no longer contain their pent-up anger. What they can no longer tolerate is the feeling of powerlessness.

A mother picks up after her children. Finally she explodes: "Why do *I* have to do this? *You* aren't crippled! How many times have I told you. . . ." Her anger hasn't accumulated. She is experiencing a progressive loss of power over her youngsters and she wants it back. Anger is the way to get it.

A teacher lashes out at his pupils for being disruptive. He has not accumulated anger but rather a loss of self-esteem for not being important to them, for not being able to do his job well.

A teenager angrily pushes open the front door and stalks into the house. "Nobody will say 'Hi' to me on campus—nobody! I'm *sick* of it, *sick* of it. I've *had* it up to *here!*" Anger hasn't been building. What has been building is one rejection after another until anger is expressed. On campus she keeps a smile on her face. She expects to be treated as she is at home, but her friendliness is misinterpreted or ignored.

Catharsis ("venting" an emotion) means attacking somebody verbally or with foam bats, pillows, or other

27

tools of therapy. For many years psychologists believed that angry people should be encouraged to vent their wrath this way in therapy, like pressurized air is vented via a safety valve on a pressure cooker. But the results were always temporary; angry victims after relief became angry again in the same situations. If catharsis worked, then people who lost their tempers in certain situations would not lose them the next time they were confronted with that frustration because their anger had been "released." The fact is, people who lost their tempers originally continued to become angry after therapy. There was no lasting therapeutic value.

This technique may be of some help, however, because it reveals to people who deny their anger that they are indeed angry. It helps them to gain insight into their true feelings. Catharsis is of value if afterward the patient has a greater understanding of what is causing the anger.

Brenda was a good example of this point. Her make-up in place, she sat primly in the clinic wearing a tailored blue dress under a broad, white collar. She lived with an uncle whom she despised but did not know it.

"You're angry," the therapist noted.

"Actually, I am not angry," Brenda replied in an emotionless tone. Her foot, however, was moving vigorously up and down.

"Why are you kicking like that?"

"I'm just a little nervous."

"Brenda, you're sitting on a good deal of rage."

"I am *not!*" Her voice was higher now. "Why are you doing this to me?"

"I'm trying to get you to see the truth."

Brenda jumped out of her chair and propped herself on the therapist's desk, facing him with a reddened face: "I am not angry! Do you hear me? I hate you! You are deliberately trying to make me say things I don't want to say. Stop it or I'll walk out that door!"

She sat down to catch her breath. With angry eyes she stared at her therapist. A minute went by as the darts flew. Another minute. Her shoulders sagged. She put her face in her hands. "Yes," she whimpered, "you're right. I am angry at my uncle. I'm angry because . . . ."

For the rest of the session Brenda recounted a list of personal desires that her uncle was frustrating. She acknowledged her own passivity concerning her uncle's domination over her life, yet she also knew she felt a certain sense of security about having her uncle in control. Rapid progress followed and in several months Brenda ended her sessions. She was unusually bright and caught on quickly when shown how to deal with her anger.

This demonstrates the best use of catharsis in therapy. It must be used to provide insights into one's feelings followed by a careful analysis of the cause and a prescription for working it out.

## Myth 6: Angry people aren't responsible for their behavior

You've heard people say "I was so mad I couldn't see straight!" or "It wasn't *my* fault; I just lost my temper" or "Don't blame daddy; he's just angry."

What are they saying? They are implying that at a certain point angry people are no longer responsible for their behavior. This is a difficult area in which to come to firm conclusions. However, enraged persons who are acting out violently give many indications that they *do* know what they're doing and therefore they limit their behavior.

An enraged husband started throwing things. He grabbed everything off the shelf and smashed it *except his favorite pipe!*

A screaming woman started to bite her husband. She pressed down hard on his hand with her teeth but did not clamp down with her jaw. She had control. She didn't really want to hurt him; she wanted only to communicate her frustrations.

A 17-year-old boy grabbed his .22 caliber rifle and started "shooting" his family members. The trigger clicked as he carefully took aim at each heart, but he had removed the bullets from the gun the day before. He was expressing his fury but he had seen it coming and emptied the chambers of his rifle well ahead of time.

There are cases in which people do lose control of their mind through rage and may not be responsible for their behavior. The court system of the United States is wrestling with this issue today. In some cases the person demonstrating anger *is* in control but is doing something bizarre for the purpose of getting some important message across to other people.

## Summary

Anger is an emotion which few people today want to claim as their own. Because they need to deny anger, many myths have grown up. These include treating angry desires as if they did not exist, calling anger by different names in order to pretend it's not anger, justifying angry behavior by thinking of it as necessary or helpful, and pretending that anger is some annexed part of us over which we have no control.

Actually anger is a purposefully chosen emotion. Only in extremely rare instances is a person "blind" with rage. In most cases, angry people can and do know exactly what they are doing and how far to go.

Anger is largely the result of unrealistic expectations. People who have realistic expectations about themselves and other people experience much less anger.

The next chapter identifies anger as more than a simple reflex. It is a complex internal phenomenon that depends upon a wide variety of aspects of an individual, including one's moods, one's stressors, one's interpretation of the situation, one's general strength of character, and one's body chemistry.

# Three

## A Response, Not a Reflex

The sprawling ranch house in the Phoenix, Arizona, suburb literally shook with the reverberations of Tom's wrath against his son Fritz. Presently the front door flew open and his 18-year-old son stumbled out of the house with his father's fist in his back.

"Don't come back until you shape up!"

As Fritz pulled his collar up around his ears Tom yelled, "Just get out of my sight!"

Tom was later remorseful and sought counsel. He moaned repeatedly, "That kid makes me so mad. . . . "

That's a common expression of anger—"He (she) makes me mad!" People see anger as if it were a knee-jerk reflex. If they get tapped in the wrong spot they get "ticked off." They have no control. Somebody just pushed their button. Others consider an angry response as normal as bleeding after getting cut. Still others see it as the printout of a programmed computer. Somebody closes the wrong circuit and *pow!* their emotional network is shorted, resulting in an emotional upheaval.

As we saw earlier, this isn't an accurate appraisal of the situation. Anger is a more complex response, not a simple reflex. We are much more likely to become angry on one day than on another. Situations in which one person becomes angry might make another person sad or happy or bring very little response.

The initiation and intensity of one's anger depends upon

- the mood at the moment;

- the presence of other stressors;

- the interpretation of the situation;

- the desires at the moment;

- one's ego strength at the moment; and

- the status of body chemistry.

## The mood at the moment

At the beginning of his fifth therapy session Hank declared, "I don't want to be analyzed. I don't want to be described. If you or anybody else criticizes me in any way I'll shoot you."

He said this with a smile, but the point was clear. On other days he could handle it, but on this particular day he was not ready to look at any weakness in himself. He had just lost his girl friend, had demoted himself to a lower-paying job, and was experiencing nagging medical problems. The accumulation of these situations in his life—the loss of security with the loss of his girl friend, the feelings of inadequacy with his self-demotion, and the feeling of imperfection in his body (which he prized)—meant he did not want to add any other stresses. These made his threshold for anger very low.

There can be daily, hourly, and even moment-by-moment fluctuations of mood. Many people generally wake up in a snarly mood, protesting the fact that they have to leave the peaceful state of sleep and face the morning. After a cup of coffee the mood of these people can be significantly different. Some become angry at night. Some experience periods of depression and anger just before they eat lunch or dinner. News on the media can change moods. One's own thoughts and memories can alter moods. Anger depends upon one's normal vascillation of moods.

## The presence of other stressors

Hans Selye, perhaps the world's leading authority on stress research, has adequately demonstrated how *stressors* in the lives of animals and humans determine the ability to cope at any given moment. Generally the more stressors (areas of frustration, confusion, or loss) in one's life, the less one is able to adapt to stressful situations.

If a person has just received a variety of good news from his doctor, his banker, his spouse, and his teachers, he will find it difficult to become angry no matter what happens. He is so optimistic that even traffic jams and discourteous people would not bother him a bit. He feels good about himself so he feels good about other people. He might go for hours and days without becoming angry. On the other hand, if he has heard bad news from his physician, his banker, his spouse, and his teachers, he might get angry at a trifling matter. He may even *look* for a situation to be angry about.

34

## The interpretation of the situation

Two husbands on a particular Tuesday evening arrive home an hour late for dinner. Their wives had the meal on the table when the husbands said they would arrive, but now it has gotten cold. Each woman is frustrated in her attempt to be a good wife.

One wife begins scolding her husband as soon as he steps inside the house, finally screaming and going to her bedroom to cry. The other wife says to her husband, "Have a seat. I'll warm up your dinner. It'll be ready in about 15 minutes."

Identical situations, quite different responses. The difference is in how the women interpret the situation. The first wife became angry because she saw the cold meal as a reflection on her worth as a cook, as a wife, and ultimately as a person. The woman who did not become angry did not see the husband's tardiness as a reflection on herself but merely as her husband's problem. She did not interpret the cold food as a reflection on her own goodness as a wife and as a cook.

*Anger is not produced by a situation but by one's interpretation of the situation.*

It is amazing how many different meanings people assign to situations. One experiences ecstasy and appreciation at the sight of a cloud-spangled sunset while another worries about rain. A teenage boy thinks pizza is the best food ever invented; his father ranks it at the bottom of the list. The men in a prayer group have different emphases and interpretations of the scripture passage that is read. No two people interpret words and phrases exactly the same way.

We do not record experiences literally as does a tape recorder or a movie film. Each interprets experiences as a painter—some more realistically, some more impressionistically, and some as abstractly as Salvador Dali. No two of us paint the same experience on our mind. Each creates experience in a unique way. This way is determined by a vast complex of our feelings at the moment, the values we hold, and our emotional responses to the various aspects of a situation. What stimulates and angers one person bores another. What brings out sadness in one person might bring out anger or jealousy in another. Indeed, one of the aspects of loving in a mature way is the ability to appreciate and value the differences between oneself and the other person.

### The desires at the moment

The first two factors which prove anger is not a simple reflex (the mood at the moment and the presence of other stressors) are fairly easily understood. The role that one's *desires* play in the generating of anger is more difficult to understand. It can be illustrated by the desire we call hunger. If a person is not hungry he is not likely to get upset if there is a long line ahead of him at a restaurant. If he is hungry, however, he might become upset about the line, even though he has no time pressures on him.

We have many desires—desires to relate to people, desires to be alone, desires for power, desires for praise and affirmation. These desires wax and wane like the restless tide. *Anger depends to a great degree upon the intensity of desires present in a given situation.*

If you have just been insulted by a bully you might have a need to feel powerful again. If you have just broken your watch and feel a loss of possession or

36

pride you might become angry more quickly than at another time. If you do not have strong materialistic tendencies, a broken watch or a torn shirt may have little effect.

If you have been ignored by people who are important to you and you want someone to acknowledge your existence and someone else snubs you or doesn't hear you properly, you might become intensely angry. But if you don't need or want affirmation or appreciation, someone's snub might not have any effect on your anger whatever.

If you are always feeling loss of power or if you interpret every situation as a power struggle, then loss of power in a conversation is likely to elicit anger. If you don't particularly care about power the same situation won't have any effect on your level of anger. If you want love or security, then the loss of a friendship or the disruption of a relationship will have significant ramifications and might elicit anger. On the other hand, if security and love are not important to you this loss might bring out only sadness and no anger.

If you are feeling overworked, underpaid, and unappreciated, you might become angry when your son asks to borrow the car. You might carry on about your poverty during your adolescence and how hard you had to work for what you got. You are not really complaining about the use of the car but you are feeling unappreciated as a provider. You feel you are being taken for granted by your son. At another time you might have recently been complimented or in other ways made to feel appreciated. Then when your son asks for the car you would readily give it to him and feel good about it.

A 14-year-old girl who is striving to overcome her own dependence on her parents so that she can have a feeling of worth and strength might come unglued and run away from home when her parents ask her to be home at a certain time. However, on another day when she is feeling worthwhile, her folks' curfew might not affect her at all. Our levels of anger fluctuate with our moods in just this way.

## One's ego strength at the moment

A significant factor which influences the occurrence of anger is how much a person needs to enhance his opinion of himself. A person who has just endured a humiliating experience might be inclined to doubt his worth and value. He might become angry with the next person who comes into his life, no matter what they do or who they are. In such cases the angry person is saying, "*You're* the bad guy; *I'm* the good guy." It's more a defense mechanism to help a person feel "OK" than a ploy to make another feel bad.

## The status of body chemistry

Good nutrition, rest, and exercise all contribute to the body's wholeness. To rob the body of vitamins and minerals is to reap effects not only in physical disability but also in psychological damage. To deprive the body of rest is to render it useless. And to omit all exercise is to hasten the deterioration of muscle and tissue.

Fatigue (whether caused by lack of food, sleep, or exercise) and anger go together. A person who attends to this trio of good health has fewer reasons to become angry.

Some people are unwittingly destroying their bodies through excesses that are generally accepted by society. One example is excessive indulgence in refined sugars. Sugar destroys the white blood cells, B vitamins, and some minerals. When the body is robbed of these essentials the nervous system is affected. Over-sugared people can become nervous, depressed, and angry. Often this is a result of a low blood sugar condition.

Another robber of steady nerves is caffeine in excess. Whether it comes from coffee, colas, or chocolate, caffeine is a culprit in robbing the human body of health. It has been established that caffeine consumed during the early months of pregnancy can cause birth defects. Caffeine in chocolate, working with theobromine (a heart stimulant), causes a rise in blood pressure and pulse rate. If this is combined with other emotional stresses, destructive anger can be the result.

Good nutrition means supplying for the body those nutrients which it needs from fresh fruits, vegetables, whole grains, and dairy products. Smaller amounts from poultry and fish complete the body's requirements. Many vitamins are fragile to light and to heat. To be safe it's good to take a basic multivitamin-mineral supplement to provide the proper balance of nutrients. If your body is deficient in its chemical requirements your emotions may be unhealthy too.

### Anger's see-think-do

In contrast to a reflex, a response goes through a process of observation, cognition, and action—like this:

| | |
|---|---|
| External stimulus: | A 10-year-old boy spills milk on the table. |
| Sensation: | Mother sees the event with her eyes. |
| Recognition: | Mother understands with her mind what has happened. |
| Memory: | Mother remembers past milk spillings and past warnings. |
| Loss of power: | Mother feels her boy is not paying attention to her values. |
| Loss of control: | Mother feels her boy is not obeying her. |
| Loss of perfection: | House is made messy (imperfect) by the spilled milk. |
| Prediction: | Mother realizes she has to stop eating, mop up the mess, and later eat cold food. |
| Anger: | Desire to attack the son. |
| Choice of behavior: | Mother elects to shout rather than to slap boy's hand. |

The above illustrates the difference between a simple reflex and the more complex response such as anger. The entire series of events in such a response can happen within a fraction of a second, making the whole situation appear to be automatic and uncomplex. Actually, however, the events that happen between the occurrence of some external phenomena and the subsequent behavior of a person are very complex and are mediated by the many psychological processes described above. Changes in any of the psychological processes bring about modification (increase or decrease) of the angry wish to attack. At any given moment one's anger response is to a large degree dictated by these many psychological internal processes. However, over a period of time angry responses can be altered (increased or decreased) by growth in areas of a person's life which lead him or her to become more realistic in his or her interpretation of the situation, wishes, and expectations of other people and things in the environment.

The following illustrates further the reasons anger develops:

| It's true, the other person . . . | But you would not get angry unless . . . |
|---|---|
| was late for an appointment. | you wanted to run by *your* schedule rather than by anyone else's. |
| made an error. | you did not want to be reminded of your own potential to make errors. |
| was dishonest. | you wanted to enhance your own feelings of goodness by pinpointing the other's sin. |

41

| | |
|---|---|
| crowded into your lane in front of you on the freeway. | you felt you owned that lane or felt you needed to be treated specially. |
| argued back with you. | you felt he should agree with your ideas; you did not want him to have ideas different from your own. |

## Summary

Owning one's anger is a valuable two-edged sword. Just as I recognize that my anger is my own response to a situation and is not caused by other people in a mechanical fashion, so I also realize that other people's anger is their own and is not caused by me in some mechanical manner. The way I behave is my response. The way people respond to my behavior is their problem, and they must deal with it. Recognition of this is a major step in maturing. Achieving the ability to let other people have their own feelings without feeling responsible for them is important for personal growth.

Anger is always a choice. It appears to be an involuntary reflex, but it is not. People who are bothered by excessive anger can learn to develop other responses and thereby enhance their lives, their relationships with other people, and their productivity.

Nobody is a helpless victim of some mysterious, irrepressible compulsion called anger.

Where does anger come from? That is the subject of the four chapters in the next section: "Sources of Anger."

# SOURCES OF
# ANGER

# Four

# The Desire
# to Feel Powerful

The first of the four major sources of anger is the desire to feel powerful in human relationships. When this desire is thwarted, anger results.

Power is seeing ourselves as free from being coerced by others. If I feel that my behavior is my own choice I feel powerful. If I feel that my behavior is determined by others I feel weak.

We desire to *feel* powerful to make up for a *deficit* of power. The person who feels powerful doesn't need anger; the person who feels weak needs anger to restore a sense of power.

Alexander the Great approached the pinnacle of power by wanting to conquer the world; Jesus Christ taught that the path to power was to want nothing: "So do not worry about tomorrow; it will have enough worries of its own" (Matt. 6:34).

Alexander said *lead* and be powerful; Jesus said *serve* and be powerful.

If you care what people think and want them to like you, you will have less power and more anger; if you don't care what people think, you'll have more power and less anger. The person who doesn't care what happens tomorrow will be powerful; the person who worries about tomorrow will feel weak because he is dependent so much on other people.

Power stems from how you see yourself, not from how you behave. The person who strives to be a millionaire will be almost totally controlled by others. He equates riches with power, believing that when he is rich he will be powerful. The truth is, when he *gives up* the wish to be rich he will become powerful.

### Power plays

In most human encounters, power is at work in the total relationship. Salesmanship places power at the center of a relationship. Books like Robert Ringer's *Winning Through Intimidation* become bestsellers. In his classic book *How to Win Friends and Influence People,* Dale Carnegie skillfully shows how to gain power over other people. Carnegie's book calls for friendliness and courtesy, giving the appearance of a developing relationship. The other person then becomes vulnerable to your influence because of a desire to have a relationship with you. The power struggle between parents and children is perhaps not as obvious but most parents and most children are well aware of it.

The so-called battle of the sexes is exploited by the media, testing whether males or females are stronger. Many arguments between spouses evolve around power. Many disagreements over money, for example, are arguments not over money per se but over the control of money.

At social gatherings games are played in conversations about trivia to enhance one's sense of power—one's ability to control the conversation, one's power to influence the emotions of another, one's skill in grabbing the attention of other people. The game of seduction is a power struggle. The goal is to get the other person to want you more than you want them. The one who wants the other person the most is the loser. The adage "Marry someone uglier than you" touches on this point.

## Autonomy and anger

Anger supports power in two ways:

- it reduces the desire to relate to others in warm, friendly, vulnerable ways and

- it intimidates others by making them afraid to use their own power.

Let's look more closely at the first point: *It reduces the desire to relate to others in warm, friendly, vulnerable ways.* Anger supports independence and autonomy by reducing one's feelings of wanting, desiring, or needing the other persons. You appear less desirable to me if I get angry at you. Result: I don't want what you have. By not wanting you or what you have I feel a greater sense of autonomy, independence, and an ability to choose freely. Hence, anger makes me feel powerful.

The second point is: *It intimidates others by making them afraid to use their own power.*

Anger supports power by warding off the power of other people. The expression "I've had it up to here," if said in an angry voice, makes other people a little more cautious. We don't like to add further frustration to an already angry person. When the person presents a veiled threat of physical or psychological harm, we appease them. As a rule, anger supports autonomy and freedom. It keeps the angry person from feeling weak.

What's wrong with feeling weak? Usually nothing. There are many situations over which we have no control. We don't have absolute control over what we feel or what we wish for or what happens to us. Admitting this is an important part of maturing. Everybody who is authentic experiences times when he or she would just like to curl up on someone's lap and weep. Christ speaks to this need when he says, "Come to me, all of you who are tired from carrying heavy loads, and I will give you rest" (Matt. 11:28).

Many times the Bible expresses God's willingness to comfort us. Realizing that we don't have as much power over events as we wish we had is a healthy acceptance of reality. Anger can give us an imagined sense of power, power that we do not realistically have. That false sense of power prevents our growth and keeps us from accepting reality.

Suicidal thoughts support power. The idea that a person can choose how and when to die offers a sense of power over destiny that some could feel no other way.

One unpleasant aspect of the death of a loved one is a sense of powerlessness. Often the bereaved one says, "I feel so helpless." The inability to keep the other person alive is depressing. Some people become angry at God, at fate, or at the medical profession in order to avoid a sense of hopelessness.

Disasters, burglary, suffering, accidents—all of these

bring a discomforting feeling of helplessness because we could not prevent them. Anger is often exhibited in such instances to avoid acknowledging one's helplessness. It promotes the myth that one is powerful: "If *I* had been there I would have stopped it!"

### Power and megalomania

Megalomania and egomania are forms of narcissism. These are often found in leaders of religious, political, or social groups—persons who have an insatiable craving for power and adulation. They always have to attempt something bigger and better in order to outdo their last achievement. Tutankhamen's building of the biggest pyramid so he could have the best possible burial place is probably the height of megalomania.

Let someone suggest to these people that they are not "the greatest" or "the most powerful," and they can become enraged. Colleagues who disagree or say no soon become ex-colleagues.

Sometimes it is difficult to tell whether such leaders are doing these things for the benefit of mankind or as monuments to their own narcissism. An easy way to determine this is to see if they become angry when they are frustrated in their desire to build bigger and better things.

Actually these are persons who have strong wishes for security and approval. Because of these wishes they feel weak. They make up for this weakness with a show of power. Their followers gain a sense of power and fame by identifying with the power and fame of the leader. This is the glue that holds cults and some mainline congregations together.

## Power and marriage

It is natural—even healthy—to experience a power struggle in marriage. Worse problems arise when spouses insist that there is no power struggle. Issues become cloudy, resolutions and solutions are avoided, anger is maintained for days, months, or years. Relationships are harmed, sometimes permanently.

Barbara berated her husband angrily for three months in therapy sessions because he had had a prolonged extramarital affair. In session after session the offended woman complained of her husband's unfaithfulness. Over and over she repeated the phrase, "How could he *do* this to me?"

Finally her anger subsided and she began to look at her reactions objectively. "The worst part of this whole thing," she said in a moment of lucidity, "is that I did my best and I could not stop him from having the affair. At first I denied he was having it, but I knew he was. My own helplessness is probably the worst feeling in the whole situation."

Barbara's anger was a smoke screen to hide her feelings of helplessness. For most of her life she had tried to control people. She was a leader in her church and a genuine asset to any group she joined. Her problem? She did not know how to relate in ways other than domination, organization, and control. The fact that she could not control her husband was shattering.

One of the most devastating aspects of rape is the victim's feeling of utter helplessness. When first approached, a woman thinks she might either talk or fight her way out of a bad situation. But when she realizes that she is going to be raped no matter what she does, her whole mood changes. This is the worst moment—helplessness; an inability to defend herself against this violation. For most women, this helpless feeling is worse than the sexual act.

Many marital jokes concerning "the boss" pinpoint the power struggle. The feminist movement focuses on the need for women to attain a greater position of power in marriage and society. Power is involved in the decisions concerning how money is to be spent, where to go on vacations, who will eat the burned toast, when the lawn will get mowed, what television program to watch at eight o'clock, and so on.

Most arguments in the home are probably struggles for power rather than merely differences of opinion. John wants to sleep late on Saturday morning but Mary wants him to clean the garage. John spends a half hour defending his need of sleep; Mary spends an equal amount of time proving that the need to clean the garage is more necessary. They both become angrier and angrier. Perhaps they really believe that cleaning the garage and sleep are the real issues. They are not. The real issue is who will have power over the other. Probably both need anger to give them a sense of power so they can win their arguments and continue to deny the fact that they are hurting because of the strain in their relationship. Each holds on to anger so the other will not take advantage. Each says, subconsciously, "I must remain angry in order to maintain my integrity and my autonomy." So they argue endlessly about important-but-irrelevant topics to maintain their anger and feel powerful.

Only God knows how many acts of violence and even wars have been started because people refuse to admit to a power struggle. Examples are everywhere: A man tells his dog to stop barking; the dog keeps barking; the man shouts at the dog, feeling a loss of power over his pet; the dog keeps barking. The man gets a club, saying: "You're going to stop barking if it's the last thing you do!"

Biblical teaching on the submission of wives to husbands seems to revolve around the issue of power. Radical feminists seem to need their anger towards men to make up for a deficit of power which they feel within themselves. Male chauvinists who emphasize the submission of wives gain power from Scripture to make up for their own deficit of power. The Bible becomes a weapon of intimidation of the spouse rather than a guide for personal growth.

Many women submit to their husbands but remain angry because they feel a significant loss of power. A person who feels strong internally does not need to be angry or to be unwillingly submissive or to coerce others by bringing in the authority of Scripture. Scriptural exhortations and suggestions should help people mature, not fulfill their own needs for power.

Probably there is no one right Christian way to resolve the location of power in the family. Each couple has to work out their resolution of the power struggle.

Some husbands want their wives to be quite independent. Some wives want to be very dependent. By discussing with each other the issue of power itself, couples can come to satisfactory solutions. If they avoid the issue of power and focus on decoys, the issue will never be resolved.

Bob and Marilyn had argued for 15 minutes about the color of their wallpaper selection. Since they had learned certain techniques of problem resolution they stopped in the heat of the argument and each asked, "What am I feeling?" Bob realized he was feeling some loss of authority over his wife. Marilyn was feeling that her husband was intruding in one of the areas over which she had control—that is, interior decorating. It was clearly a power struggle of which wallpaper was merely a symbol. Once Bob realized that she was not trying to intrude on his authority, but merely to hang on to what little power she had, the color of the wallpaper became relatively unimportant. She assured him that she wished him to remain the boss but wanted a few areas to express her own personality.

Issue resolved. Marilyn got her choice of wallpaper; Bob felt unthreatened.

### Power between parents and children

Parents and children play games with power. The rise in child abuse is evidence of that. How much grief could be spared if these parents accepted the fact that they cannot always control their children as they wish. But because their own sense of power is so tenuous it is easily threatened, and the parents rage at their off-spring rather than allow themselves to feel helpless.

A 2-year-old child resolutely answers no to every demand; an 8-year-old is consistently late for dinner; a 13-year-old refuses to cut his hair—these youngsters are demonstrating the power struggle between parents and children. Parents who become angry at such behavior are also demonstrating the power struggle.

Children possess a strong drive for autonomy and independence—the power to choose. It is important for the character of children that they have a realistic sense of power.

Morality is based in part upon one's independence from other people's wishes and desires. Immorality is often a sign of dependence upon others. People are often willing to do things they know are harmful and wrong just to maintain a relationship. Autonomy is a necessary goal of growing up. On the other hand, too much autonomy leads to a frustrating life because there is no satisfaction from being with people. Intimacy and close communication help children to find a balance between autonomy and warmth. Helping a child find *that* is the most difficult part of being a parent.

When a child says in one way or another, "I'd rather do it myself," he is involved in a power struggle. Such children are strong and parents shouldn't quench that drive. The best way for children to gain a realistic appraisal of their own power is to let them do a lot of things by themselves so they can test their strengths and learn their limitations.

On the other hand, children often have fantasies of power well beyond their capabilities. To protect their children, parents must at times stop them from doing exactly as they wish. There is no absolute answer as to when to let them try and when not to. It's time to say no when there is danger of physical and psychological harm. It's time to say no when the child is doing things that are contrary to important values of the parent.

Some parents resolve the power struggle by giving the child all the power. This liberality produces a child who thinks the whole world will treat him as his parents did. He fails to recognize the importance of taking care of other people's needs and desires. Some parents resolve the power struggle with their children by never allowing the children to have any power. They intimidate, intrude, and generally leave the child with poor self-esteem. The danger of this is the development of a dependent child who will be unable to make good moral choices as an adult.

Many people misunderstand the strong-willed child and the stubborn adolescent. The strong-willed child is usually combatting what he sees as his biggest weakness—dependency. The parent interprets it as rebellion. Each comes at the problem from an opposite viewpoint. The fact is, most rebellious children are overly dependent. These children appear to be rebellious by merely trading their dependency upon parents for dependency on their peers. The peer group becomes the parent figure. In rebelling, the teenager uses anger to counteract his or her feelings of weakness and dependency. Truly autonomous people, because they are *not* overly dependent, do not need to rebel.

## Unsolicited power

Others sometimes give us power that we don't want. For example, a professor will ask his class to garner two ideas from a certain book. A zealous student reads the entire book and turns in a lengthy report. The professor is unhappy because he has to read more work than he assigned and the student is angry at the professor for giving him "all that work."

Students who work excessively long hours on homework, employees who spend evenings working at the office, wives who work themselves to the point of fatigue in order to entertain their husbands' friends—these are all examples of persons who attribute to these other people great power and influence. In many cases they work harder to please the person than the person wishes.

Why do they do it? Most often to be deeply loved

and appreciated. They are saying, "Some day, if I am good enough (or smart enough or strong enough), I will be recognized and given special treatment."

We view other people as powerful *if* we know we cannot coerce them. The more one is independent from others, the more powerful one feels. A desire to please others first is a desire to have power over them. The desire to feel powerful results from a deficit of power. Anger is an attempt to get it back.

## Summary

The desire to have power over another is a major source of anger. It must be resolved before the angry person can be delivered.

The drive for power is useful and productive until it interferes with the desire to relate to others in warm and friendly ways.

A contented person is not one who has everything but one who desires nothing.

The journey from anger to contentment consists merely of a change in attitude.

# Five

## The Desire
## to Feel Self-Sufficient

When people or situations imply that we are inadequate for the task, the common response is anger. It can be seen in people from kindergarten to the grave, from the time a child wants to put on his own socks until the senior citizen wants to write his own will.

Who hasn't heard: "Buzz off, kid, I'm in charge here!" or "Don't baby me, I can get my own breakfast!" or "You're telling *me* how to cook when I've been doing it for 20 years?"

Self-sufficiency and dependency are opposite poles of this continuum. Denial of one's dependent, needy self is our most common case in the clinic. Psychotherapy begins its constructive phase when people are prepared to admit that they are needy, and not until then. People who struggle hardest for self-sufficiency are the most dependent. They have not yet overcome feelings of dependency left over from infancy.

Nobody is totally self-sufficient. We need other people to build our houses, manufacture our cars, process our food, sew our clothing, refine our fuel, filter our air, educate us, protect us from enemies, and solve our disputes in court. In almost every area of life we need help from somebody else.

The illusion of self-sufficiency prevents people from going to doctors when they need help, from seeking counsel when they are ignorant, from weeping in front of their friends, from admitting financial need. One of the biggest resistances to faith in God is the illusion that we don't need his salvation ("I can do it myself!" or "I'll take my chances").

In contrast, some of the high points in marriage or in any other relationship occur when we humbly admit to the other person our inadequacies. We strain our relationships when we struggle to hide shortcomings. For example: How many wives would like to be included in their husbands' careers but are left out and made to feel unnecessary? (A note to threatened spouses: If you dare to admit weakness, your spouse will love you more, not less. He or she may admire you less but they will love you more. Humility costs, but it pays.)

## Who's on first?

Jim, a company executive, had control of 52 employees. He was an excellent boss. His people respected him. He was known as a competent leader, a good guy, a high performer. Neither he nor his wife were able to understand why Jim was so different at home: crabby, dictatorial, full of complaints, yelling, screaming—in general, the opposite of the good-guy image he presented at work.

When counseling started, he said that the reason he acted better at work than at home was because his employees obeyed him and his wife and daughters didn't. He tried to dig deeper into his anger toward his family. Typically he wanted to see his anger as *their* problem.

Jim discovered that at a deep level he was unnaturally dependent upon his wife. More than he realized, he wanted to please her and he wanted his wife to be as accepting, encouraging, and affirming to him as he was to his employees. In other words, Jim wanted Linda to be his supportive, ever-loving boss.

She, on the other hand, was confused. She acted toward him as she would toward a dictator—with fear and trembling, as though he were self-sufficient. Underneath she sensed his deep dependency. He would often ask her for advice and rarely stood up for his own opinions when she dissented. It took Linda quite a while to realize that his domineering was designed to hide his need of her. What he really wanted from his wife was tenderness and love, but neither he nor she recognized it. She was fighting for her own survival in front of a "tyrant." He complained and nagged to get her to provide more leadership. The two of them had spent 18 years in their unsolvable pattern until he grasped the fact that he really was not self-sufficient. He desperately needed his wife.

Linda was so shocked and surprised at his basic dependency that she could scarcely believe it. When Jim admitted it, with tears flowing down his cheeks, she could not resist his weakness. For the first time in their married life she said, "This guy *needs* me!" That gave her worth. She found significance and value in the marriage. She no longer needed to fight for her life; she *was* important to him. But it had taken a long time for both of them to recognize it.

## The "self-made" person

Prosperous people sometimes fall into the trap of thinking that they alone are responsible for their success. They picture themselves as King Midas—everything they touch turns to gold. The truth, were the "self-made" person able to admit it, makes this cock-a-hoop braggadocio appear ludicrous.

"The thing that I like best about my wife is that she never bothers me," said a proud business executive in Minneapolis. He honestly believed that he was a man who needed no one, and he fancied that his wife was without need also. He had several secretaries, several yes-men as vice-presidents, a custom tailor, a personal acquaintance with several maitre d's at fine restaurants, a valet, and a private pilot. This man pictured himself as the head of this supportive parade, yet said (and believed), "I don't need *any*body!"

He saw all of his servants as extensions of himself. He was under the illusion that he owned these people because he paid them. He could not see them as individuals; he saw them all as one unity. He pictured himself as totally self-sufficient, but in reality he was trapped by his intense desire to have all his needs met instantaneously.

The late Howard Hughes fell into this trap. He had several personal physicians and a cluster of valets and bodyguards. Eventually, who becomes the master? Men and women in these pits of their own making have to live a tight schedule to maintain the illusion that they don't need anybody. They cannot tolerate the feeling of needing someone, so before they let themselves feel needy they order someone to take care of that need. Unfulfilled need is intolerable. It is demeaning. It makes people angry.

A wealthy person, since he or she "buys" people, can maintain the fantasy that he or she is doing it alone and needs nobody. Even the working man can cling to that idea. "My wife is making my dinner because I told her to. Therefore, it's not she who's taking care of my needs, it's me!"

What arrogance!

A government worker took his bride to Washington, D.C., where they settled down at a low position on the groom's career ladder. His wife got a job to help pay the rent on a medium-priced apartment and they were happy.

Approximately one month after the wedding the bride's father visited them and decided the couple was not eating as well as they might. He didn't like the absence of color in their cheeks, and proceeded to give them advice on how to eat. He added insult to injury by leaving a $100 bill behind so they could "buy some decent food."

When people give advice, the implication is: "You're not able to figure it out for yourself." That insult produces anger.

### Loving comes hard

Self-sufficient people have a hard time loving and being loved. Tenderness threatens their self-sufficiency.

A common problem presented to marriage counselors is the difficulty one partner has in reaching orgasm during sexual intercourse. Typically, if one brings it up the other becomes defensive and angry. The implication is, "You're inadequate." This goes against the desire to be self-sufficient in everything and the result can be anger.

A certain degree of self-sufficiency is good; it can foster independence and prepare a person for many tasks. But a desire for complete self-sufficiency can hinder relationships. For example, people who strive to be self-sufficient are usually loners who have a hard time working with others.

These people on a deep level are searching for people to take care of them. Therefore in subtle ways they are demanding, but on the surface deny their desire to be taken care of. When this desire to be coddled is frustrated they remain mildly angry. Since they refuse to admit their dependency neither they nor the people around them understand their anger.

## Self-sufficiency and parenthood

Parents, especially fathers, try to appear before their children as all self-sufficient. This is an unrealistic goal. Parents who find this tendency in themselves should reevaluate who they are. These parents tell their children things like: "It's a hard world out there; you gotta be tough to survive." "Don't trust anybody." "Don't cry." "Stick your chin out; you can take it!" "Don't let anyone see weakness in you. If they do, they'll tear you apart like wild dogs."

These and other myths about self-sufficiency are perpetuated upon children who, if they believe these messages, will be in trouble as adults. Fortunately, children don't always believe these ludicrous statements and easily recognize that admitting one's dependency upon other people both emotionally, physically, and spiritually is central to a wholesome life. A person who can't trust other people can't trust God either, because a refusal to trust other people is a refusal to admit one needs help.

Young mothers often have difficulty accepting help in taking care of their children. One mother who came to the office declared with a certain pride, "I've never had a baby-sitter for my children." Here was a mother who had very little gratification in her life. She was afraid to admit she needed a rest now and then. If God needed the seventh day to rest from his creative activities, perhaps mere humans need at least that much. We *can't* do it all. We need vacations, rest time for our own pleasures, and, most of all, a willingness to call on other people for help. Some, of course, go to the other extreme. They act out their dependent selves so much and ask for help so often that their helpers become angry. Hypochondriacs are typical examples of persons who always use their needy parts but never their adult parts. There needs to be a balance.

What can parents do with children who are too dependent—who reveal their infant parts more than their grown-up parts?

First, recognize that these children are refusing to live up to their age. They are refusing to leave the dependent, infant stage.

Second, look at your own needs to fulfill their wishes. Why do you need to be all-sufficient—the rescuer? Are you trying to provide for your children what you basically want other people to provide for you even now as an adult?

Third, before you do anything else, spend several months talking to a friend, counselor, or spouse about your own dependency demands. Generally parents cannot adequately cope with demanding children until they have outgrown their own dependency needs. This results in a growth-producing situation in which the children's demands no longer bother mother or father and the children are free to grow into the next stages.

"Empty nest syndrome" is a major problem to mother and sometimes to father when the children leave home. Parents who suffer from such a syndrome are parents who have not been in touch with their own dependency needs. They have become overly dependent upon their children.

Some parents rush their children out of the home before they are psychologically ready. These parents are narcissistically oriented—they resent anything or anybody that interferes with their own gratification and have little interest in the gratification of others. When problems arise they would rather kick the kids out than go through the long process of compromising some of their own wishes.

How much independence shall we give our children? There is no exact answer to this question because different children need different amounts. In general it is best to give children as much freedom as they can handle without doing great damage to themselves and others. Usually, but not always, children will live up to what is expected of them. If we treat them responsibly and trust them they are more likely to act responsibly. The more decisions we are able to leave up to the children the better.

Parents smother children, not by doing too much for them, but by not paying attention to their wishes. Something bad happens when parents ignore the child's individual characteristics and do what they want for the child. To make a child learn to ride a bike before he or she wants to is smothering. To prevent him or her from riding when he or she wants to is also smothering. It all comes back to how much you love and care about the child's wishes, values, and integrity. The same treatment might be smothering to one child and not to another. Pay attention to a child's wishes. Smothering is often done by parents who would rather follow rules than relationships.

## When healing begins

It is an exciting time in therapy when people finally say to themselves: "I now see what I have wanted from people all along. I was subtly demanding that they be gentle, comforting, supportive, and protective of me. In essence I've wanted them to be my parent figure." (Married persons often expect this from spouses.)

Recognizing this source of anger results in two things:

• A realization that one will never get his or her deepest wishes fulfilled. This brings sadness.

• A recognition that people are important even though they can't act as parents. This brings love.

People react to these realizations by saying, "My God, what have I been expecting?" They experience feelings of genuine guilt. Often spouses go home and apologize. They accept the fact that they'll never get their wishes fulfilled. Loving comes hard when you make demands of people which neither you nor they recognize. People always disappoint.

Nobody is going to take care of us as much as we wish. Many suicides involve not an escape from life but an escape *to* a new existence where "I will be taken care of forever."

## Summary

Anger is a response that people choose rather than face their feelings of helplessness and dependency. They would rather become angry than realize their limitations.

People who are not afraid of feeling helpless at times have no need to be angry when their helplessness is presented to them. They do what they can about a situation and feel no remorse over what they cannot do.

> *God grant me the serenity*
> *to accept the things I cannot change;*
> *courage to change the things I can;*
> *and the wisdom to know the difference.*

# Six

## The Desire to Feel Important

The last two chapters showed how anger grows out of the desire for power over others and the need to be self-sufficient. When these two desires are unfulfilled, anger is one response. The anger does two things:

- It gives people the illusion that they indeed are powerful and self-sufficient;

- It helps people avoid the painful truth that they are not as powerful and self-sufficient as they wish to be.

The desire to be important, significant, or popular is a third desire that triggers anger. Wanting to be first in line, president of the club, captain of the team, chairman of the board, or the winner at everything are some of the thousands of examples illustrating this desire.

The more I need to be important to other people, the less secure I feel about my real importance. The more I brag and strive for status, health, and prestige, the more likely it is that I feel insecure about my own importance and will become angry when my importance is threatened. These importance-seeking activities are designed to help me find significance in the eyes of others to make up for the significance I lack in my own eyes. If I am not supported in my quest my response is either anger or a combination of anger and sadness called depression.

## What makes us feel important?

Importance comes from having our emotions acknowledged. Many people think that importance comes from having *behavior* acknowledged. If someone says to you, "That's an excellent paper!" you may feel good but you don't feel that you are known by that person. If, however, instead of reading your paper a person listens to you and understands your feelings about the topic, you will experience the thrill that leads to the expression, "Gee, he listened to me! Not to my product but to the *me* behind the product."

*Being understood is more affirming than being praised.*

What is the real "me"? Is it my ideas? My looks? My behavior? My talents? No, at the very heart of "me" are my desires. As long as people acknowledge me for my ideas, looks, behavior, or talent I feel rejected. But when people understand my desires and also my fears of not getting my desires, then I feel understood.

## How low self-esteem begins

What makes a person feel like a nobody? It would be easy to assume that people suffering from low self-esteem grew up in large families where they were ignored and not listened to. This usually is not the case. More often those with low self-esteem were the center of their parents' attention. The more attractive they were, the more attention was paid to them, not only in the family but in every group they entered. Soon they learned that a distinction is made between how a person feels inwardly and how he behaves outwardly. When inner desires and outward behavior don't agree, a person feels most likely a nobody.

Let's state that another way: When people behave toward us on the basis of our performance and do not pay attention to our inner selves, we feel insignificant. For example, a talented youngster comes skipping into the house as visitors arrive. "Come here, Sissy," says her father. "Play the piano for our friends."

"No, daddy, I don't want to," Sissy replies shyly.

"Oh, come on! Play it anyway. You're good. They'll like it."

Sissy quickly gets the point: her performance is important, her feelings are not.

Ultimately, our view of ourselves is not what we do, it's not how people respond to what we do, it's not the outward show. Our view of ourselves is what we *feel* and *desire*. The core of how we view ourselves is the seat of our emotions. Until you have acknowledged a person's feelings you have not acknowledged them at all.

Does this mean it is always best to give in to another's desires to help their self-esteem? Of course not. For one thing, it would be bad for *your* self-esteem. More importantly, acknowledging one's feelings is not the same as giving in to them. To say to a child "I understand that you want me to buy you a bag of pop-corn" is not the same as buying the popcorn. Simply tell the child, "I know how badly you want the popcorn but I do not want to buy it for you at this time."

The child's feelings have been acknowledged and although the child might be angry, he or she will not feel loss of self-esteem. Loss of self-esteem comes when our feelings are not important enough to be heard.

People who have a good view of themselves are per-sons who feel comfortable with the emotions they pos-sess at the moment. They feel that their emotions are OK. They distinguish between emotions and behavior. They can easily say to themselves, "I feel angry . . ." or "I feel sad . . . " or "I feel happy . . . " or "I feel like jumping up and down for joy." They are fully aware that they can control their behavior to make it appro-priate for the situation, but they are not ashamed of their feelings.

For example, a husband came home from work one day and freely said to his wife, "I was humiliated today at the meeting. The boss blasted me in front of the other vice-presidents. I was so angry I felt like leaving."

The man was angry, but he feels important enough to want his feelings heard. He has no expectation that his wife can or will do anything about his feelings except understand.

But what if his wife had not acknowledged his feel-ings? Suppose she had said, "You have no right to be angry! Your job pays well. The president has done you a lot of favors, and lots of men would love to have your job." Then that man would have felt small and discouraged because his feelings were disapproved.

## Bigheadedness

On another occasion the wife of the man in the story above was in a whirl of happiness when her husband arrived home from work.

"Howard, I was chosen to lead the 'Fiesta Days' Parade next Saturday. I'm so happy . . . this is the first time ever that I feel a part of the Thursday Club's executive committee."

She needed only her husband's warm affirmation at that point. But what if he had countered with: "That's no big deal. Don't get so bigheaded about a little thing like that!" She would have been crushed.

People who are "bigheaded" are not those who have been praised excessively but those who have had their feelings go unacknowledged. Bigheadedness is the desire to find importance by exterior means to make up for the unimportance we attach to our own feelings.

It's impossible to praise too much, provided in the praise the person's feelings are understood and acknowledged. Understanding the feelings of another does not necessarily obligate the listener to change his or her own feelings or to do anything. Many tensions in relationships would be resolved if people could acknowledge each other's feelings yet feel no obligation to do anything about it.

For example, two brothers had a bitter argument. The older one remained angry for several days and was impossible to live with. The father in his wisdom sat down and heard the older brother's viewpoint. After 40 minutes of talking the older brother felt better and once again became tolerable to live with. The father felt no need to change anything or to confront the younger brother.

Merely to sit with someone who has suffered the loss of a loved one or who has become ill, even if one sits there silently, is enough to restore their feelings of importance because their feelings are heard. People feel important when their feelings are heard, understood, listened to, and empathized with.

People who are sure of themselves feel that their emotions or desires are satisfactory. People who have an unsure view of themselves are those who do not approve of their emotions or desires.

A child's responses to acknowledgment begin at the breast. Case studies show that some mothers hold the baby at a distance even while the infant is sucking; other mothers hold the baby too close, so that the nasal passages are almost blocked; still other mothers have a beautiful sense of oneness with the child, hugging and giving space as the child needs it. When the child's wishes and feelings are acknowledged he has a better start, a happier childhood, and a more enjoyable adulthood.

Many people avoid questions about how they feel. You ask a young preacher how he is and he might reply, "Great! Why, when I came to this church there were only 100 members. Last Sunday after only six months, praise the Lord, we had 500 at the morning service."

First of all, he didn't answer the question; second, he came close to blasphemy, pretending to describe what God did but down deep taking full credit for the progress and growth.

His true feelings probably were: "Things are going great. I feel good about what I have done here in a few weeks. I've worked hard and the people like me."

This second answer is authentic—there is nothing

71

wrong with being proud of one's achievements. But perhaps this young man was giving himself more credit than he deserved. Perhaps he was not really glorifying God. Does he have an obligation to be perfect in all of his thoughts and feelings? Of course not! By being authentic two things happen:

• He expresses his true feelings and both he and his listener know they have communicated honestly. Their relationship is deepened.

• He may become aware of his pride and try to grow in this area. If he hid his feelings he would be less aware of areas in which he needs to grow.

## Anger and loneliness

The saddest part of living alone is the feeling that "No one cares if I live or die." Lonely people don't necessarily seek fame, glory, wealth, or power; they merely want to be assured that someone knows of their existence and cares.

In many cases, lonely people have exaggerated views of their own importance and a derogatory view towards their own feelings. They often say: "If people knew how great I was they would pay attention to me." On the other hand, they are ashamed of their anger, their desire to be with people, their tenderness, and their aggressiveness. They sit day after day waiting to be rescued by someone from their own awfulness.

Sylvia, 25, divorced, and beautiful, complained of a lack of male companionship. "Why don't men like me?" she moaned.

This young woman had a history of dating passive males whom she dominated and manipulated. She, of course, denied her manipulation. In therapy she finally got in touch with her fear of being dominated by males. As the best defense she had taken an aggressive offense. When she confronted her fear and worked through it unashamedly she had less need to dominate and ultimately became engaged to an outstanding partner. She had been ashamed of her fear of men so she had never dealt with it.

Rene was an attractive but lonely girl. Throughout her teen years and early adulthood she was known to the boys as "nice-but-dull." She couldn't understand why a person who cared so much and listened so intelligently was bypassed for the more aggressive types.

In therapy, Rene recognized her fear of being assertive and associated it with a domineering father. She was so ashamed of her own assertiveness that she instead acted supersweetly. In therapy she acknowledged and accepted her assertiveness. She now is glad to bring her assertive parts into her relationships with men and she's more fun. Guys appreciate her character and the fact that she stands up for her own feelings. Her social life is greatly improved and she feels much more important as a person. Loneliness subsides and the feeling of importance increases as we acknowledge our feelings.

### Anger and status

Disciples James and John were thinking of importance when they asked of the Lord, "When you sit on your throne in your glorious kingdom, we want you to let us sit with you, one at your right and one at your left" (Mark 10:37). The apostles sought the highest level; Jesus gave them a proper perspective! "If one of

73

you wants to be first, he must be the slave of all" (Mark 10:44).

God's way of evaluating character reveals that those who do not care about being important in the eyes of others have the highest character and the greatest spiritual development. Peter was action-oriented, not feeling-oriented. He couldn't even face a maiden and admit who he was.

To seek status is to be perpetually angry.


## Anger and public image

The quest for importance is a dead-end street. The more you want to be important, the more people detect the facade and won't pay attention to what is really going on inside you.

To make up for a lack of affirmation of their real selves, people try harder to act important, hiding more and more deeply the real people inside. This splitting of the real person inside from the behavior outside is the dynamic that leads to making a person feel like a nobody.

Take the case of a college student known on campus as "the preacher boy," a young man with outstanding powers of persuasion. Other students would call on Dave to witness to their friends or family because Dave had been used by the Holy Spirit to influence many toward Christianity. He worked so hard to live up to his reputation as an evangelist that his learning, social life, and personal meditation and growth suffered.

"I'm an empty shell," Dave told the school counselor. "I'm spiritually bankrupt."

He had enough insight to know that while he was

influencing others toward increasing their faith he was desperately trying to convince himself. He recognized that his "great spiritual giant" image was indeed quite the opposite of the real inner Dave. The rift between the outside man and the inner person was great.

As a "spiritual giant," he found himself alienated from the rest of the students. Nobody dared to talk to him about such mundane things as the basketball team scores, the laundry, what he was feeling, and what his struggles were. His isolation deepened and his anxiety increased to the point where he was willing to give up his reputation and willingly expose his real self to the counselor. It had been a long time since anyone had listened to the real Dave, since anyone had paid any attention to the real feelings of this young man. Finally, Dave experienced himself as a nobody.

As he allowed himself to experience who he really was, he began to feel more and more like somebody. His need to maintain his reputation diminished. His willingness to be real with the other students increased. The reputation of the evangelist diminished while his capacity for warmth and love increased. He had been a victim of his own search for importance. Only when his desires and feelings were acknowledged could he be free.


## Summary

We are fortunate if we have someone who values our inner person, someone who judges us more by our inward desires and feelings than by our outward behavior. Then a secure self-concept is possible. Until we believe that our inner person is significant, complex, and knowable, we will continue to be angry. Our environment will suggest that we are less important than we want to be. Unless we have someone who values our wishes and emotions on a continuing basis, we will continue to search for unrealistically high places of importance and experience the anger that comes from not being in those places.

A mature person is one who does not depend upon the opinions of others for happiness. To such a person, a task well done is more important than the feelings and approval of others. A mature person is willing to be last in status because he is first in terms of character.

# Seven

# The Desire
# to Be Perfect

*If it's worth doing, it's worth
doing poorly. Think about it.*

—Keith Edwards
Rosemead Graduate School of Psychology

The last three chapters have examined anger as a response to loss of power, anger as a response to loss of self-sufficiency, and anger growing out of thwarted attempts to feel important. This chapter looks at anger resulting from a loss of imagined perfection.

The straight-A student becomes angry and depressed when given a B, the concert pianist is upset over a single error at the keyboard, the baseball player throws his bat when he strikes out, the homemaker cries when the biscuits burn, the salesman fumes at associates because the department's average dropped during the quarter.

Is this passion for perfectionism exaggerated? No, despite the protestations of these frustrated perfectionists. Although they protest, "But I really don't want to be *perfect* . . . ," a deeper look reveals that perfection is exactly what they demand of themselves. They think they have to become perfect in order to be accepted.

Perfectionists are always disappointed by their performance, no matter how good it is. If they do 99 things right and commit one error they are upset. Perfection is indeed their goal, even though they protest, "Nobody's perfect."

## How perfectionism begins

Young children have few standards. They cannot tell whether they are good at putting on their socks or bad, whether they are good at nursing or bad, whether they are good at crawling or bad, whether the feelings they have of hunger, pleasure, or anger are good or bad.

What they do experience is pleasure while being held, while feeding, while being gently talked to, while playing with their toys, while being relieved of unpleasant stimuli such as dirty diapers and sharp objects. They associate pleasant and unpleasant feelings with what they are doing when these feelings prevail. These children have had enough tenderness and acceptance to know the pleasure they bring. They find, however, that acceptance is hard to come by. It happens only rarely. They feel unaccepted while nursing if mother is irritated about having to nurse them. They sense by her voice, her movements, and the way she holds them whether they are accepted by her.

Youngsters are thrilled when they first walk, but parents want a few more steps and the thrill is gone as the children struggle to comply. This happens hour by hour, day by day.

On a subconscious level children learn not to enjoy the things they do in order to please their parents. They learn that when they are angry, they are mildly rejected; when they are happy they are tolerated but their elated feelings aren't acceptable.

A boy races into the house excitedly and cries, "Mom, look at my frog!" But mother reacts negatively: "Take that slimy thing out of here! You'll make a mess!"

A girl builds a house of blocks and she's pleased with herself. Mom observes, "That's nice, dear, but you'll have to clean it up before supper."

A child makes something from a glob of mud. "Look, Daddy, at my mud cow!"

Daddy responds: "That's not a cow. Cows don't look like worms."

Children soon learn that nothing is totally pleasing. Therefore, they can't fully enjoy anything they do or anything they possess.

Other emotions that are not good enough are desires and needs. A three-year-old girl wanders into the kitchen and announces, "I want a cookie."

Mother immediately registers anxiety. "You can't have a cookie, dear. It's too close to supper. You'll spoil your appetite."

"I want to stay up late," she says at the age of five. Father registers anxiety: "Baby, that's not good for you. It's bad for your health." Instead of implying that the child's behavior is inappropriate, he implies that her *desire* is inappropriate. The child concludes that *wanting* is an unacceptable emotion. She learns to deny what she wants in order to live up to what she thinks she ought to be.

This is the key to anxiety in children. They perceive that their parents think everything the children wish for is immoral. When mother is afraid to say no and experience the inevitable separation from her child that answer brings, she becomes anxious. It sticks out all over. Children read this clearly and conclude that it is wrong for them to want *anything*. This is, of course, not the message that the mother was communicating. But the result is that children experience a sudden break in their relationships rather than a simple denial of what they want. The children decide: "Better not wish for that anymore. It must be morally bad."

The focus here is on relationships which revolve around how other people appear to us—their emotions and feelings toward us. To a large degree, children's views of themselves are determined by what they believe their parents think of them. If they sense that their parents are anxious, they conclude from their ego-centered perspectives that they are the cause of the anxiety. They feel a loss of warmth, a loss of relationship. If asking for something makes mother anxious, children conclude, "I did something wrong."

Children blame themselves for their parents' feelings. The youngsters then try to control their parents' feelings by acting in ways that calm the parents. They want to avoid making the adults anxious. Maturing is growing up to realize that you are *not* responsible for the actions of adults. We are responsible only for our own actions and feelings, not for the actions and feelings of others.

Children who are perfectionists relentlessly try to find ways to keep their parents and other adults calm, accepting, and unconditionally loving. Their utopia (being loved without having to earn it) is to be so good that finally their parents accept them. They long to achieve what they think are their parents' standards so they idealize perfection. To reach that impossible stage they are continually striving, striving, striving. Alas, they inevitably fall short and have a deep inner sense of failure: "I am not good enough." These children are superobedient because they learn, "If I do everything mom tells me to, she won't be mad. I can't stand it when mom and dad get mad."

## How perfectionists respond

When people or situations interfere with the perfectionists' goals, they respond with anger. This anger most often is of a mild, chronic type, but it can also be rage. Extremes can be spotted in these three examples:

The doorbell rang. "Pardon me, sir, but your son threw dirt clods on my lawn and I want him to pick them up immediately."

Most people would have smashed the clods or let them dissolve in the next sprinkling rather than have an angry confrontation with a neighbor over a minor issue. However, this man's lawn and landscaping were perfect and he strove hard to keep them that way. Any blemish made him anxious because it interfered with his desire for perfection. A perfect lawn was more important than relating well with the children of the neighborhood.

*Crash!* went the picture window of the ranch house as a car squealed away from the curb. At the wheel was John, a man who was very proud of his car. He washed it weekly, or even more frequently. While it was parked in front of his friend's house a sprinkler was turned on and his car was soaked. Rather than tolerate any blemish on his prized possession, he became angry and threw a rock at the offender's window.

"I'm sorry, I can't help you any more," Marilyn fumed and slammed down the receiver.

As secretary to the vice-president of a thriving company she had a deadline to meet and became anxious over the possibility that she was not going to make it. Anyone who interfered with that goal became the object of her wrath. Part of her job was to take phone calls and to talk with clients. Another part of her job was to prepare a daily summary of accounting charts. The closer she came to the deadline for the completion of the charts, the more angry she became with people who "interrupted." Finally Marilyn became rude and insensitive to callers who were not to blame for her deadline or her anxieties.

Marilyn felt in some deep sense that if she were to miss her deadline, she would be less than the ideal secretary. Those feelings were intolerable. To get rid of them she blamed other people. "It's *their* fault for interrupting. I'm trying to do a good job but they won't let me."

She could have taken the phone off the hook or asked an associate to help, but that would not have been playing the role of the perfect secretary and she was not willing to do it.

People who have a strong need to see themselves as perfect are, of course, greatly offended when criticized. Their usual defense is to attack and the battle begins:

"I think you're spending too much money eating out," the wife charges.

"It's my money; I earn it; I can spend it however I wish! And furthermore, you are spoiling the children by giving them whatever they want. You give in to their every wish."

For the next 10 minutes this not-so-untypical couple debated about who did the best job of misusing money. Finances was only one of many topics that could have been debated. The real issue was, "Who's worse—you or me?" Each of these people had a strong need for perfection and rarely did they communicate with each other without attempting to prove that one was worse than the other. Any possibility of enjoying each other had long since been eliminated.

Growth will be very slow for these people because of their refusal to realistically view their own motives and fears. Each one is literally terrified of discovering his or her own normal, selfish, dependent, imperfect self.

These people are terrified of discovering imperfections in their characters because they assume these imperfections are as repulsive to God and other people as they are to them. So they live with the myth that they really are as "good" as they think they should be. They become angry when anyone suggests anything less than good about them. The truth is they will be more lovable and more able to love if they give up their wished-for selves and accept their real, complex, multi-motivated persons.

## Saved, sanctified, and neurotic

Jesus' injunction to hunger and thirst after righteousness is sometimes used as a support for perfectionism. But those who are "perfect," those who think they have attained righteousness, are least likely to hunger and thirst after it. We can't hunger and thirst for something we already possess.

Christ was speaking to ordinary, sinful people. People who face their imperfections are more likely to follow Christ's injunctions. When criticized, nongrowers defend and attack. Growers remain fully open to the possibility that the criticism is justified. Growing people don't have a need to depreciate others in order to maintain their own goodness.

Some people are chronic confessors. They regularly (almost eagerly) admit to their personal weaknesses and failures. They give the appearance of being thoroughly honest regarding their own imperfections. Chronic confessors are motivated by the urgent need to ward off criticism by others. In other words, they confess openly to a lesser evil to distract themselves and others from more painful disclosures. Chronic confessors tend to have an exaggerated, grandiose, privately held view of themselves; they use their confessions as decoys.

Any time we think that a problem we have is someone else's fault there's a good chance that we have an unrealistically high view of our own selves. Tom consistently views his teenage sons as the cause of the only unhappiness he experiences in his life. He considers himself to be without problems. Unfortunately, teenagers tend to live up to their parents' worst expectations, and his sons provide a lot of examples Tom can point to. The fact is, Tom is so afraid to admit his own faults that he spends most evenings and weekends attacking, criticizing, and in general trying to help people discover their shortcomings. Needless to say, the family is not too fond of being around Tom. Tom's need for perfection is so intense that he even refuses to admit he's hurt because his own children actively avoid him.

## Who's to blame?

Don't blame interrupters. They are usually not conscious of the load of care they are placing on the perfectionist.

Don't blame parents. Even though parents might be "perfect" in deed and character, children err in the way they imagine their parents, then respond to what they imagine.

Don't blame mates. One partner will love the other more without the illusion of perfection.

There is only one person who is responsible for perfectionism and all its tentacles—the perfectionist. He or she must endure the humbling experience that leads to giving up the fantasy. He or she must become broken in spirit and lay aside the quest. "Tribulation works patience." One kind of tribulation is the realization that we are not as perfect as we wish we were. Furthermore, we don't need to be.

Anger is a protest. It is saying, "You're not treating me as I should be treated. You're interfering with my climb to perfection." The angry person must face the truth to overcome anger. Truth leads to sadness (depression) without anger, but the sadness is temporary. Joy follows when we get relief from the pressure to perform, when we realize we don't have to be perfect in order to be acceptable. "Nothing . . . nothing . . . will ever be able to separate us from the love of God" (Rom. 8:38-39).

## No shades of gray

Most perfectionists characterize the world as either right or wrong, black or white, cold or hot, up or down. Every situation tests their perfection. If someone disagrees, one of the two has to be wrong, one right. The perfectionist naturally defends his position—openly or inside his head.

But many issues discussed in everyday living have neither right nor wrong answers. They are matters of taste and preference, not of morality—the brand of coffee you prefer, the ball club you root for, your choice of cars, the way you decorate your home, your church denomination, your hairstyle. However, if a friend or passerby implies that a perfectionist's view is wrong, this angers the perfectionist. The perfectionist is impatient with other people's views. "The idea! She serves that stupid Coffeemate when *any*one knows Cremora is *much* to be preferred."

"Children should be spanked! The Bible says so," Betty fumed in her women's prayer group.

Imogene objected: "But you're supposed to love and nurture them."

"But the Bible says they will be spoiled if you don't," Betty responded, tension growing.

Soon rational discussion ceased and hard feelings developed. Certainly spanking is an issue worth discussing, but it is possible to discuss an issue, have differing opinions on the subject, and still feel loving toward each other afterward. Although on one issue there may be strong differences of opinion, we can recognize agreement in hundreds of other areas.

However, for the perfectionist this is *not* possible. If one idea is not totally perfect and acceptable, those old fears of imperfection revive and anger results. "If I'm imperfect in one part I might be imperfect in all. I'm not good enough. . . ." There's no recognition that they might be partly right or partly wrong in a certain situation, or right on some issues and wrong on others.

Probably neither Betty nor Imogene could tolerate the possibility that their strongly held beliefs should be questioned. The bottom line was: "If you don't accept my ideas I feel as though you don't accept me." They failed to realize that they could disagree without damaging their friendship.

## A perfectionist's fears

A perfectionist's bigger fear is the loss of the wished-for self and the emergence of the person he is afraid will be unmasked—i.e., one who is totally bad. The fact is, we're all mediocre in most areas. The victim of perfectionism lives daily hoping for the best and fearing the worst. He sees the two extremes. To surrender to realism would be to slide into the terrible state of being mediocre. To the suggestion that there is nothing wrong with being mediocre the perfectionist reacts with shock and resentment. To him, anything short of perfection is bad. It's either total agony or total ecstasy. There is nothing between Egypt and the Promised Land. The concept of growth is not even considered.

People who have a relatively normal view of themselves see each situation realistically and don't read into it any more than is there. They realize that every situation is only a small fraction of their total life and therefore do not let any single event threaten their feelings of being OK or acceptable.

When they are depreciated, persons with less healthy

views of themselves have two choices: they can be devastated and depressed or they can become angry. Anger is a way of rejecting the self-depreciation while at the same time avoiding the devastating and equally unrealistic feelings growing out of an exaggerated view of one's worthlessness or badness. Anger, then, is often used to support an unrealistic view of oneself and the world. Anger is a substitute emotion used by people who have unrealistically high and unrealistically low opinions of themselves.

## Perfectionism in marriage

Martha married young but medical problems caused her to be childless for six years. Those were wonderful years—Martha and her husband Luther doing things and going places together.

Luther was completely domineering, but Martha accepted it and catered to his whims. Finally Martha bore a child and eventually they had a second.

The children brought tensions into the home and took Martha's time. Martha could no longer pamper her husband, so he reacted angrily. His loss of importance grew as Martha concentrated on raising the children. Luther turned to his hobbies, seeking compensation for his loss of significance in the home. As dissatisfaction grew, Martha sought help in a therapist's office where her story unfolded.

After the wedding, Martha thought Luther was perfect. She also considered herself to be an equally perfect wife. In order to maintain this myth, she denied any imperfection in him and in herself. This fulfilled Luther's fantasies and covered over any problems in their relationship which threatened to break through the facade.

Her purpose in visiting a therapist was to learn how to overcome her husband's indifference toward her and the children. She denied that she had any anger but she spent every session berating her husband. It was a year before she would admit her anger and deal with it. By not admitting her husband's imperfections, those imperfections were never dealt with. By wishing to believe in her husband's perfection, she slowed down the deepening of their relationship and the building of character. Both Martha and Luther avoided facing the realities of who they were as a couple and as individuals and avoided the developing problem—their relationship. Anger on both sides was the inevitable consequence. They wanted everyone in the church, community, and family to see what a perfect marriage they had. In truth, their union was deteriorating rapidly. Their relationships were cold and unfulfilling. Each was in love with his or her image of the other; both were in love with the persons they *wanted*.

### Perfectionism and the family

The excited father sat on the edge of his chair, his hands gesturing wildly. "Of all people in the world, the members of our family should be the most warm and accepting. But they're not. Relationships have sharp edges. There are crosscurrents of misunderstanding, even hate. What's wrong with us?"

First of all, what's wrong is the father's expectation of a "perfect" family. Notice his choice of the word *should*. Somehow he has the fantasy that people really can live that harmoniously. When human beings live closely together (each wanting pleasure, attention, importance, and power), perfect community is impossible. As long as the father continues to compare his reality with his perfectionistic fantasy he will be disappointed with himself and with his family members. The wonder is not that we have imperfect relationships; the wonder is that flawed people get along at all.

Television, family how-to books, and many novels present a completely unrealistic view of family life. The Bible is much more realistic about people. Adam and Eve and their children, David's clan, Solomon's family—all of them give a true perspective about the human heart and its possibilities for evil.

## Summary

Anger is the chosen response of people who have deep needs to see themselves, and to be seen by others, as perfect. In situations which prevent them from being perfect, anger is their response.

Any person who criticizes a perfectionist is likely to be attacked.

Rather than use frustration and criticism as part of self-evaluation, perfectionists become angry. This anger ranges from annoyance to rage.

Perfectionists can change only by admitting that they are not perfect and never will be. They need to recognize that others will love them more in their admission of imperfection than in their fantasy of doing everything without a blemish.

# DEALING WITH ANGER

# Eight

## How to Handle Anger in Others

"One more temper tantrum and my daughter's going out for adoption. . . ."

"My teenage son seems to be angry all the time."

"My wife wakes up angry. Something is bugging her but I can't tell what it is."

"My husband is always angry when he comes home from work."

"My boss picks on me. I can't do anything the way he wants it. . . ."

Anger in other people makes us anxious. We feel afraid, helpless, and sometimes angry ourselves. Eight general principles are useful in defusing angry people who are acting out their anger:

1. *Determine the source of the anger.* Get a clear picture of who owns the anger. The source of anger comes from inside a person, not outside. Don't believe people when they blame their environment, their circumstances, or other people for their anger. Rage in people is their problem, not yours. It is caused by their frustration, not by yours. It is their response to life, not

yours. If acting out anger is what they want to do, that's their problem, not yours. Do not accept responsibility for their choices.

2. *Remain separated from angry people's emotions.* When people around you are angry, you do not need to become like them. Separate yourself mentally by saying, "This is his (or her) problem; I am not going to make it mine." Sympathetic anger is of little value to anyone.

3. *Don't accept blame.* You are responsible only for your behavior, not for the feelings and behavior of people around you who are angry. Others may choose anger to keep from feeling weak, helpless, imperfect, and insignificant. You may have been mean, thoughtless, rude, or uncaring, but their response to your behavior is theirs. If you're sorry, apologize for your behavior, not for the other's feelings or response. To say, "I'm sorry I made you angry" is ridiculous. Instead, say: "I'm sorry I stepped on your geraniums."

What if the other person still becomes angry? That's his or her choice. You can change or refuse to change. Regardless, the other person's anger is his own.

4. *Determine what their anger is covering up.* Find out what the other people are substituting anger for. Is it to avoid a loss of power, a loss of self-sufficiency, a loss of importance, or a loss of perfection? Ask them what they'd feel if they did not feel anger.

5. *Refuse to be a "garbage dump."* Angry people often feel cleansed and purified internally after acting out their wrath. They may expect you to act lovingly toward them after they have heaped abuse upon you. Do not allow it. Do not live up to their expectations

by being all-loving, all-forgiving. If they want to dump verbal garbage on your head do not permit them to expect your docile response. It doesn't do either of you any good.

6. *Don't augment their fantasies.* You have no obligation to respond to any angry person's demands to change. You do not have any obligation to help them change either. You may or may not wish to do so. That's up to you. The point is: don't feel obligated to help them make their fantasies come true. Face them with reality.

7. *Determine what anger they are projecting.* What are these angry people projecting onto you or onto someone else so they can escape blame? Refuse to see yourself as bad in the way they want you to see yourself. Remain separate from this angry opinion of yourself.

8. *Help them to "synthesize."* Accept others' anger. Tell them it's okay. But don't tolerate abusive words or behavior. Say: "You're angry, and that's all right. But don't expect the whole world to get angry with you."

Give them feedback. If your feelings were hurt, say so. If you felt like leaving, say that. Don't suffer in silence. Angry people don't realize what negative consequences their behavior has on others. Most people see their anger as an asset to help them get what they want. If no one tells them it's a liability instead of an asset, how will they know? They might otherwise continue to believe that other people see them as powerful, important, self-sufficient, and perfect.

Now let's turn to some descriptions of people around you and see how the eight general principles can be applied.

## Angry infants

Many children enter this world complaining. Soon it becomes a habit. For some, it is characteristic for a lifetime.

Rage in the first six months of life is a special problem because of the little one's inability to communicate his discontent or to understand his parents' response. Some rage is inevitable and probably healthful. But excessive rage in infants may lead to emotional disturbance in later years.

If infants experience too much discomfort they will learn not to trust people to provide comfort and safety. This will spoil their warm relationships in later years. The preverbal memories that are stored by rageful infants will haunt them for years.

Since infants' survival depends upon others, being left alone is a serious threat. Most infant rage is related to the terrifying feeling that they are left to their own inadequate powers, therefore their survival is in doubt. It is extremely important to give comfort, cuddling, care, and attention to rageful infants. That's sometimes the *last* thing parents want to give because these babies are so full of rage. When parents don't know what the infants are raging about, they feel helpless. This can become so stressful that the parents strike back in anger. It is better for adults to embrace their raging children and learn to tolerate the feelings of helplessness.

The causes of infant rage are most often unknown. Physical discomforts such as colic, fevers, excessive gas, and hunger, as well as dreams, unidentifiable discomfort, and fears can contribute to infant rage.

Ella, a schizophrenic 18-year-old, grew up in a family that had good emotional health. The girl had some colic during the first 12 months of her life, and she raged continuously day after day. On the advice of their family doctor, her mother left Ella in a room and closed the door. Ella's dependency in adulthood was the result of those lonely, helpless feelings in babyhood.

Children who are not frustrated grow up believing that people care enough to comfort, support, and help them when they need it. They do not feel desperately helpless. On the other hand, children who are frustrated in obtaining their basic needs (food, fluid, safety, comfort) grow up with the attitude that people cannot be trusted ("Only I can take care of myself"). These persons lack the capacity for intimate love that is necessary for gratifying relationships.

All children are angry at times because their world is not as they wish it would be. However, not all children express their anger. For those who do, there are four ways parents can help them to get rid of the frustration:

1. *Remember that anger is not bad.* It is inevitable and necessary for growth. Anger can be a valuable catalyst in helping children to become mature individuals. Some children become angry following a misunderstanding. In their anger they experience alienation from, and a diminished dependency upon, their parents. Each of these little incidents takes children one step further from the infant-mother relationship of the good old days. The more they remove themselves from mother's wings, the more potential they have for individuation and maturity.

2. *Directly address children's anger.* Say, "You seem

to be angry." This will help them identify the emotion and also let them know that it is OK to be angry.

3. *Help them focus on solutions rather than merely ventilating.* Getting angry doesn't do any good unless it leads to constructive action.

4. *Limit their acting out behavior through verbal control and physical restraint if necessary.* When a child is angry and goes to his room, parents should feel positive—it is a sign that the child is developing a more realistic view of the world. To say to a child "Don't be angry" is ridiculous and fruitless. Being angry is both necessary and inevitable for growth in human experience. Children instead need to be taught to use their anger in constructive, not destructive, ways. They need to realize that feeling anger is OK, but breaking things, hurting people, or verbally attacking people is out of place and will not be tolerated.

The causes of anger in childhood are essentially the same as those in adults. Anger is a protest because the world is not the way we want it. Anger blames the world to avoid lowering one's expectations.

If anger helps the development of children, why does the Bible say, "Do not treat your children in such a way as to make them angry" (Eph. 6:4)? The difference can be illustrated:

If natural events frustrate children, they can learn to be more realistic about life. But if *people* frustrate children, they do not know what realistic expectations are. For example: If a child's tower of blocks falls over because he stacked them unevenly he has no one to blame but himself. If his father *kicks* it over he blames the father and doesn't learn anything about realistic expectations.

97

If this happens often, children will come to believe that their frustrations are generally the fault of someone else and out of their control. This causes the development of a mistrust or hatred of people and an inadequate sense of control over their environment. Therefore, adults should not tease, taunt, or purposefully frustrate children. The Bible is interested in growth, and no growth can come of such provocations; they can only increase hatred.

## Angry adolescents

The most frustrating aspect of the teen years is young people's unjustified anger at parents and teachers. We call it unjustified because we don't see any reason for the intense anger that teenagers exhibit. Why do these young people, especially in the post-puberty years (ages 12-16), become so angry? The answer is simple: They need their anger in order to separate from their parents.

Adolescents must change their view of themselves from children to adults. Most have a strong need to reach back for the security of their old parent-child relationships. However, this insults their need to be powerful, independent, and self-sufficient, so they vacillate. Teens who are most dependent on their parents need anger to feel grown up. Adolescent rebellion is in essence rebellion against the old parent-child relationship. The ones who feel least adequate deny these new feelings and substitute anger in their place. Runaways, truants, dopers, delinquents, and others who are acting out anger generally feel inadequate in their ability to cope with the adult world. Anger gives them a temporary feeling of strength.

Another large generator of anger is the need to blame others. Adolescents who have not enjoyed successful experiences feel powerless, guilty, socially out of place, and inadequate with the opposite sex. They devalue others to bolster themselves. In the process, they attack and condemn other family members and people in general. They feel better for a while, but it leaves parents bewildered, wondering what they did to deserve such outbursts.

If you are parents of such adolescents, review daily the eight suggestions at the opening of this chapter. In addition, confront these young people about their feelings of inadequacy. Take the time to understand the events in their lives (usually social) which lead to their lowered self-esteem and subsequent angry outbursts.

Teens readily admit inadequate feelings to an adult or peer who accepts them. It is important to reiterate to them the damage their attacking outbursts do to your feelings and other people's feelings. Tell them this behavior hurts and will not be tolerated. If you say nothing and take the abuse, the outbursts will continue and the child will keep projecting blame. Once again, feelings of anger are OK. Destructive use of anger is unnecessary and unacceptable, as in this true story:

Betty screamed, "I'll *kill* him!" and bolted across the room toward her younger brother. Her father grabbed her around the waist and held her tightly while she raged about the imperfections of her brother. "He's selfish, spoiled, and always gets his way. He has no respect for my property. . . ."

Her father held her for several minutes until her anger lessened. When she was able to be reasonable, the brother was dismissed from the room and the father and daughter had a long talk. The father listened carefully to her complaints and gradually directed the conversation toward her relationship with her girl friend. Betty had experienced a number of social disappointments and her feeling of self-worth had been diminishing for several days. Some of her specific complaints regarding lack of privacy were justified. Steps were taken to improve the situation.

The father empathized with her social life but of course was not able to do anything about it. The father pointed out that her angry outburst was not condoned and even if her parents had been unfair it was not her job to correct them. It ended with feelings of mutual respect. Betty's feelings had been acknowledged and respected. Her destructive behavior was condemned. She realized that she could not always be treated as she wanted and that was growth producing.

Another true story illustrates a young person's passion for independence:

Paula and her father found themselves shouting insults at each other. The duel ended abruptly when Paula was slapped on the face and told to get out of the house. "No daughter of mine is going to act that way in my house!" yelled the father. "Get out and don't come back until you're ready to act like a human being."

He had just brought her home from the police station where she had been taken after being stopped on the freeway with opened beer cans in the car. Paula spent the next couple of nights at a girl friend's house. She was surprisingly at peace when she came to the counselor's office for her regular appointment.

"I don't care about him anymore," she said of her father. "From now on I'm going to live my own life."

She had successfully blamed her parents for her own inadequacies and her father had lived down to her expectations. She now felt relatively good because her father had fulfilled his role as the bad guy. It was a temporary victory, however. Her feelings of inadequacy and inferiority remained. Paula realized sooner than most the actual dynamics of that explosive evening. She was a dependent girl but disliked that part of herself. So she consorted with rebellious peers to gain a sense of independence from her parents. Being taken into custody was a thrill. It gave her status among her peers. Paula's father completed her triumph with his irrationality. Fortunately, Paula had character enough to ask her parents' forgiveness and permission to move back home after approximately two weeks.

The experience produced growth in Paula's life. Unfortunately, her father maintained his defensive position and refused to admit how much he cared. So the relationship was not as fulfilling as it might have been.

"I can't stand this house! Don't you ever tell me what to do again," stormed Jim. These words were a clear indication of the teenager's frustration, but his parents were too busy defending themselves against the insult to catch on.

His mother shot back, "As long as you live here you will do as I say! And furthermore, you mow that lawn and empty that trash like I told you yesterday."

The dynamics are understandable. Jim was fighting to overcome his child view of himself and mother was angry over her loss of power. These feelings are normal but they put individuals on the attack rather than enabling them to confront each other and express their honest feelings. Mother and son ended their battle in typical unresolved fashion—both angry, both blaming the other, neither understanding what the real problem was. The husband and father was made to be the bad guy—Jim's mother ordered her husband to send their son to his bedroom. Jim concluded that his mother's only intent was to dominate him and make him a child again.

Adolescents grow best in an atmosphere of honest expression and mutual trust. Parents would do well to remember this if they desire to maintain good relationships with their children during the teenage years.

## Angry parents

Thousands of children live day after day with an angry mother, an angry father, or both. Many a father or mother comes home from work frustrated and unfulfilled. They are unable, because of their own fears, to deal with problems at work, so they redirect their anger at their families. Children take a lot of unfair abuse because of parents who are unwilling to deal with their anger at its source.

What can children do if one or more parent is excessively angry? Some parents are angry only when they're drinking. Many children say, "My dad is good when he's sober but when he gets drunk, it's hell."

It's almost impossible for children under the ages of 13 or 14 to confront their parents about behavior. Children's representations of who they are and who their parents are almost preclude any responsible confrontation, although this can be done and should be encouraged if the children are strong enough.

Generally, however, confrontation of parents by their

children is unsuccessful. It's very difficult for angry parents to admit any weaknesses to their children. For children who have angry parents we suggest this approach:

Recognize that your parents' anger is not a definition of who you are. If they call you a "no-good beggar" that is a comment on *their* feelings, not on your character. This is hard, but very necessary. Some children can do it quite well.

A gifted five-year-old boy whose mother was schizophrenic could in a very realistic and healthy way ward off his mother's anger with the explanation, "Sometimes she gets crazy and doesn't know what she's doing." In this way he protects himself from her accusations and still maintains a positive attitude towards his mother in general.

A 12-year-old girl consistently says of her mother, "She is in one of her bad moods today." She uses this to disregard her mother's angry outbursts. This is a necessary and helpful approach to a difficult situation.

## Angry spouses

Millions of American homes are chronically traumatized by an angry husband or an angry wife or both. Inevitably the member who acts out anger does not see that this anger is changeable ("I'm just that way and others are stuck with it").

When a spouse pouts, initiates temper tantrums, sulks, throws objects, and criticizes, the other should apply the eight principles listed in the first part of this chapter. How sad it is when other family members believe the messages the angry person sends. It's better to ignore manifestations of anger, to treat them as if they did not exist. Let the person go into his snit. When it is over, carry on as before.

If there is an unresolved problem, do not let the angry person avoid the issue by displaying anger. Take the attitude: "You have the right to feel however you want, but that doesn't solve anything. Now if you've finished your acting out, let's get back to the issue and try again."

Give your spouse some feedback. State how you felt during the emotional upheaval. If you were hurt, say so. If you were angry, say that. If you felt humiliated, express that also. Too often angry people never get feedback on how they come across to others because the people around them are terrorized. They are often quite unaware of how others respond to their outbursts.

If your spouse becomes physically or verbally abusive, leave. When it is safe, return and force the offending partner to discuss what is behind the anger. Don't let the abuse go unchallenged. Continually ask what your spouse is feeling besides anger. It is rare when discussions of only anger and blame lead to anything constructive.

Respect a person's right to sulk and pout. But when the sulking is ended, the damages will be lessened in the long run if the offended party brings up the issue again. In many cases, humor ends sulking quickly. One husband began mimicking the drooping face of his sulking wife. His contortions touched her funny bone and she laughed. In another case a wife told her sulking husband, "Honey, I've got to hand it to you. You picked the *best* time to sulk. What a marvelous thing that was!"

The sulking ended with wife and husband laughing heartily. Many pouters continue their sulking longer

than they want to because they don't know how to
stop.

## Anger in public

The expression of marital anger that is probably the
most devastating to the other party and the most difficult to stop is criticism in public. Criticism always
hurts. It always leaves a scar and always is unacceptable, no matter how noble the motives of the critic
might be. But criticism in public is the sharpest barb.
All couples should enter into a pact never to criticize
each other publicly. If either partner feels criticized in
public that feeling should be presented to the other
partner.

The offender might insist, "Honey, I wasn't criticizing, I was just teasing you!"

"Nevertheless," the other party should respond, "it
hurt me."

Make your feelings known even if your partner
didn't see a hostile or angry expression on your face.
This will increase empathy and lead to more sensitivity
the next time you're together in public.

Caution: Give feedback for the purpose of regis-
tering your feelings, not as a demand that your partner change. Not expecting change is the best way to
bring about change.

## Anger in private

Disagreement is inevitable in any marriage. Partners
in any relationship cannot agree all the time. Often the
central issue in an argument is a mask for what really is
bothering the persons involved. If a couple argues and
criticizes each other for months, even years, and never

resolves the problem, it probably means that they do not *want* to solve it because each needs something to be angry about.

Dell and Marcy argued continuously about his choice of attire. She considered his clothing gauche and tacky. He considered it comfortable and individualistic. In therapy, the underlying issue emerged. He was an efficient businessman who kept impeccable records and had a well-organized life. She was jealous of his good organization and was thrilled there was one area where he was less neat than she was. If he *had* dressed neatly she would have been sad about losing the one area where she felt superior. He, on the other hand, felt dominated by his wife. He felt intimidated in most areas of his life because of his needs to be taken care of but chose clothing to express rebellion.

He needed his wife to pick on him so he would have something to rebel against. She needed to pick on him so she could feel superior. Deep down neither wanted to solve the "problem." This couple came to realize how they had conspired together to maintain areas of conflict and avoid problem solving. They now can laugh about this dynamic. If a problem persists in a relationship it is probably because both partners need it and would miss it if it got resolved. Here are some typical examples:

• A wife of an alcoholic husband *needs* someone to take care of; the alcoholic himself both resents and needs his wife's maternal attention.

• A husband both enjoys and hates a nagging wife; he hates the nagging but it gives him ample justification to stay away from intimacy.

• A divorcee complains of her husband's lack of attention to their children while at the same time hopes he stays away so she can maintain her view of him as the bad guy.

## Anger on the job

What can you do with an employer who constantly berates you or in subtle ways blames you unfairly?

Remember first of all that you are in that person's employ by choice. Outside of prison, no one is forced to stay in a position that is hated. Change is sometimes difficult and money often needed so badly that a move is threatening, but it is not impossible. Every employee should realize there is someplace where his or her skills are needed and wanted, even if it is not at the current place of employment.

Some people see themselves as victims of circumstance. These people generally need to be angry at an authoritative figure. Until people see themselves as "choosers" they will remain "victims."

Gain information by questioning other people in an objective way—do not try to manipulate the answers. Do they view the treatment you get in the same way you do? Do they see you as a victim or a scapegoat? Do they perceive your boss as being generally angry?

Once you understand the true facts about your situation, present your feelings to your boss in a tactful manner. Don't begin with an accusation. Say something like, "I have the feeling that I'm being picked on. I feel that you don't like me, that I'm not appreciated here for what I can contribute."

In most cases, a low-key confrontation will resolve a problem. Sometimes there will be a logical explanation for the boss's behavior. Sometimes there will be an altered pattern of behavior when your boss knows how you feel. Sometimes you, too, will find pleasant ways to change your outlook and consequently your attitude.

Some bosses will, of course, feel accused and become angry. In such cases there may be an opportunity to pursue the problem at a higher level of management or through your personnel department. A transfer to another department might be possible. If all attempts at resolving the issue are blocked, the option of resignation is always available. No job that fosters excessive frustrations, resentment, anger, and a lack of gratification is worth it.

Bill was a brilliant computer programmer. He worked 15 years for a company and, although there were no major frustrations, he felt unappreciated, imprisoned, uncreative, and unfulfilled. He finally synthesized enough of his feelings to resign and go into his own consulting business.

The first months were rough, financially and emotionally. But after two years he began doing extremely well. He now feels more independent and is getting gratification by being responsible for his own work instead of always being secure within the company affirmation. From every standpoint it was a move for the better. It's a pity that more men and women don't go into business for themselves. What being your own boss does for a person is much greater than most people realize.

## Angry peers

Roommates, co-workers, neighbors, or schoolmates who are angry—all these can cause frustration, depression, and loss of gratification. What can we do with peers who are angry? Again, the first principle is: You always have the choice of leaving the situation. Some predicaments are intolerable because of the immaturity and recalcitrance of other people. Not everybody is dedicated toward growing. Not everybody is dedicated toward making life easier for those around them. In many cases it is not worth waiting a decade while the other person gets his head together. You always have the option of removing yourself. It might be hard, but it is important to recognize the freedom that is yours.

*Gather the facts.* Function as a lawyer by assembling the facts as a test of your perception of the situation. Ask for the other's opinions. Sometimes it's wise to drop hints about your feelings toward the other person. Use statements like "You seem to be angry" or "I feel like your punching bag" or "Being with you is like making love to a porcupine." The person's reaction to these statements will be valuable—it can help you determine the validity of your assessment as well as the probability of the resolution of the problem. If the person angrily denies any responsibility in his behavior, the chances are reduced for any resolution. If the person becomes curious or shows a desire to explore more fully, the prospects for resolution are higher.

*Confront.* Once you have gathered data and have your perception of things fairly well organized, it's time to present your feelings and thoughts to the other person. It's important to synthesize your aggression, to use caring, tenderness, and empathy with your anger. Don't make exaggerated statements and don't make the other person feel as though your only motive is to attack. It is important the other person recognize

109

that your continuing motive is to resolve your own feelings, not manipulate or coerce him or her.

A confrontation often dredges up something that happened in the past that has been an irritant and never forgiven or forgotten. Perhaps you borrowed something and never returned it. Perhaps some gossip was passed around the group which caused hurt. Perhaps your children, your wife, or your husband made a bad judgment. Often confrontation can bring out and resolve a long-standing source of anger. In most cases confronting in a synthesized way can bring about more positive feelings between two people.

Sometimes the differences are more difficult to resolve. Perhaps your roommate doesn't value a clean room; perhaps your neighbor insists it's his right to play his stereo at full decibels; perhaps your co-worker feels he has a right to smoke without interfering with your right to clean air.

Compromises are in order. Perhaps your co-worker might agree to smoke only at certain periods. Your neighbor might agree to turn down his stereo at certain periods of the day or night. One such problem seemed insoluble until the quiet neighbor bought the stereo-playing neighbor a set of headphones. It cost him $20 but he felt it was well worth the expenditure in terms of peace and quiet. Another man realized the value of compromise and bought a neighborhood teenager a muffler for his motorcycle. It cost him $12 but it was a bargain.

Two people living in the same vicinity cannot always have total freedom. Compromising one's wishes and gratifications at times is the price we pay for the value of living with other people.

If the resolution stage is unsuccessful at solving an

110

issue of anger in another person, there are legal channels open as a last resort.

## Dealing with temper tantrums

A temper tantrum is a purging of the feeling called anger. It dislodges anger from inside the person and places it outside, leaving the insides in a "purified" condition. Temper tantrums, ironically, are produced by persons who cannot tolerate angry feelings.

Temper tantrums in children and adults are widespread and quite bothersome. In adults, temper tantrums include pouting, the silent treatment, and hypochondriasis, as well as the easily recognized explosion of violent temper.

For example, Rod exploded verbally and sometimes physically at his wife on a regular basis. This often occurred while they were preparing for sexual intimacy. Once he had unloaded his anger he felt extraordinarily good about himself and could then make sexual advances toward his wife. He could not understand her hurt feelings and lack of readiness for intimacy. He often asked, "Hey, I'm no longer angry! Why do you reject me?" (Never mind that he had just called her a whore and slapped her around.)

Rod usually arrived home angry and that interfered with warm feelings toward his wife. He felt unclean inside. He externalized these unclean feelings by vilifying his wife. This relieved his tension and he felt clean again. The anger was now no longer a part of him. He saw himself as all good. The fact that his wife could not see him as all good confused him.

The dynamics behind his anger were simple. Rod was a man with a powerful build but with little

111

strength of character. He often felt psychologically powerless. His mundane job made him feel powerless all day long. To have sexual intimacy with his wife upon whom he was quite dependent increased his feelings of powerlessness. To restore power he intimidated his wife, denied his dependency on her, and saw the relationship as once more restored. He was then ready for intercourse. After being beaten verbally, and sometimes physically, Rod's wife was hardly in the mood to be loving.

Temper tantrums allow people to get their own way by purging out feelings of anger. They then feel powerful again. Usually the victims of the tantrum are so uncomfortable that they acquiesce and the people with the temper gain the victory. Mothers with children in grocery stores say no to a request for a Popsicle or candy bar but yield when a child throws a temper tantrum or threatens one. A temper tantrum gives children and adults a temporary feeling of great power.

The techniques of dealing with tantrums in adults and children are well known and effective. The only reason tantrums do not end is a lack of strength on the part of the victims to follow these necessary steps.

1. *Recognize that the other person is not out of control.* The things they do are carefully planned. They hear you and can respond if they want to. It is important to them that they appear to be out of control, thereby relieving themselves of responsibility for their bizarre behavior.

2. *Ignore their tantrums.* When possible, simply walk away. Both children and adults are stopped in this manner. If you cannot ignore a tantrum, stand and watch it with an amused smile, as if to say, "My, what

a spectacular performance!" If they become destructive in their desperation they might need to be restrained, but do this only as a last resort.

3. *Acknowledge their anger.* When the performance is over, say, "You certainly seemed to be angry."

4. *Don't allow their behavior to change your plans.* Life goes on, and their temper tantrums should not work as a manipulation.

5. *Discuss their feelings preceding and during the tantrums.* Help them to recognize that what they wanted was OK, but that the timing or the amount demanded was inappropriate. Emphasize "inappropriate" and "unrealistic" rather than "bad." Emphasize that you accept them as people even though their angry behavior was not acceptable.

These techniques will work. The hard part is ignoring the bizarre behavior and being strong enough not to yield.

# Nine

## How to Handle Anger in Yourself

Overcoming anger is a gradual process accomplished best with the help of a mature friend, spouse, or therapist. The person you select to help should be someone who is not afraid of his own anger, who understands that anger is a normal aspect of personality, who looks upon anger as a reaction to frustration and a substitute feeling. The helper should not be afraid of your anger nor should he treat it superficially. The helper should think: "I know you are angry; I know you see your anger as dangerous; I know you have deep feelings behind your anger of which you are not yet altogether aware."

Anger is the desire to attack. This desire we call an emotion. An emotion is different from behavior. When a person experiences this emotion there are three possible responses: acting out, repressing, and synthesis.

### Acting out

The first response is to act out the anger—to attack physically (hitting, throwing, spitting, kicking, etc.)

or verbally (swearing, chastising, teasing, criticizing, pouting, clamming up, arguing, etc.).

People who act out anger are demonstrating several things. For one, they are showing that they have a difficult time handling their desires. In order to get rid of a desire (which they consider a bad thing), they act out. This removes the desire and they no longer feel like bad people. They are now rid of their anger. Anger makes one tense. Many people cannot tolerate the anxiety that accompanies anger. Acting out relieves the tension.

## Repressing

A second response to anger is repression of the unwanted emotion. In acting out, the feeling is externalized; in repression, the desire to attack is not even experienced. People who repress their anger do not experience it.

Bobbie was a sweet, helpful, loving Christian girl. All her life she heard people talk about being angry but the closest she ever came to the emotion was to feel "upset" with things.

"Honestly," she confided, "I really do not know what it means to get angry."

Bobbie was proud of this special virtue. She felt superior because she had not stooped to such loss of control. Her stepfather had a terrible temper and was angry most of the time while Bobbie was growing up. In order to avoid being like her stepfather, Bobbie did not allow herself to experience this emotion.

But the girl was only fooling herself. She developed a nervous disorder and was pencil thin. In stormy situations she took great care to calm everyone. Bobbie was easily manipulated by her friends and family who took advantage of her quite regularly. Rather than becoming upset she took pride in following Christ's command to "turn the other cheek."

The day came when Bobbie exploded. She totally became unglued and verbally lashed out at her roommate with such intensity that she frightened herself as well as her roommate.

"What has happened to me?" she asked her counselor. "I'm having bad dreams about being chased by monsters. I'm attacking people. Am I becoming evil?"

In therapy, her counselor was passive. This noble, conforming girl subtly began to plead and ultimately tease the therapist for being so unhelpful. After about two months Bobbie could no longer stand it. She found out she had a good, healthy temper.

"You're just sitting there!" she fumed. "I'm paying you to help me and you . . . you . . . . "

"You seem to be angry," the therapist commented. He smiled and Bobbie began to laugh. She had exploded in anger and was still accepted. She did not have to be manipulated anymore. She had fantasized that everyone would be frightened by her anger if she let go, just as she had been of her stepfather's.

Bobbie was able to free herself from a fear of her anger. There was some acting out, but she was able now to deal with her anger in a much healthier way.

Repression of anger comes in many forms. The major form is denial, like Bobbie's. In denial people refuse to acknowledge their desire to attack. They describe themselves as anxious or a little "tense" but the desire is not acknowledged. Ask them, "Are you angry?" and they will reply, "No. Bothered a little, maybe. Perhaps just a bit upset. But not angry." If confronted they justify their feelings by blaming others or their environment or God. Their body systems, of course, continue to secrete the hormones of an angry person and they experience fatigue, loss of sleep, headaches, muscle tension, nervousness, and sometimes actual organic defects such as ulcers and colitis. These physical symptoms may increase and decrease but their bodily reactions remain as long as they repress their anger.

Why do people repress their anger? We have found three major categories of dynamics behind repression:

• People are afraid they will act out their desires and cause harm to themselves and others.

• To have angry feelings is to be immoral, sinful, bad, naughty, or some other negative self-concept. Conclusion: Being angry is something that only bad people are. Since they can't stand to see themselves as bad, some people won't allow themselves to be angry.

• If they are angry, people will think they are repulsive, unacceptable, and intolerable. Since they don't want others to see them in that way, they hide their anger, therefore making themselves much more attractive and lovable.

### Synthesizing

A third method of handling anger is synthesis. This is the heart of the whole book. Synthesizing is the act of combining anger with other aspects of one's personality. This exercise occurs day by day, week by week, and in some people moment by moment.

This is the healthiest way to deal with anger. It mainly involves a subconscious process of modifying and channeling the desire to attack with such things as love, morality, judgment, one's own needs, fear, and reality testing.

A relatively healthy personality does not need his anger in order to feel powerful, self-sufficient, important, and perfect. He has given up those exaggerated fantasies and accepted realistic strengths and weaknesses. In such a person anger becomes a very useful motivator.

Examples of synthesizing anger most obviously include sports such as boxing, football, and hockey. Anger caused by the threat of intimidation or losing is combined with concentration, practiced skills, judgment, fear, and a desire to play within the rules in a productive, exhilarating sport.

People who cannot synthesize their anger are unable to perform on superior levels in sports even though they may have excellent natural ability. They cannot tolerate the threat of loss of self-esteem that comes from competition and they choke or blow up. Synthesized anger helps athletes to improve concentration, endure, and perform objectively. A controlled attack of one's opponent is a basis for high performance.

In less obvious ways, anger is an ally for many other endeavors of relationship, preaching, problem solving, business decisions, and personal growth.

## Psychotic episodes

The clearest examples of unsynthesized anger are those rageful psychotic episodes we read of in the newspaper. Some previously mild-mannered citizen goes crazy and shoots or stabs or crashes into things or people. Others see this as inconsistent with the pre-episode personality, but actually it is quite consistent. These persons repress their anger and as a result feel weak in relationship to others. They tend to be ignored, put down, and discounted because they cannot synthesize their anger enough to stand up for their own rights and opinions. Although they appear mild and even saintly, they are also dull and rigid. Their feelings of weakness, unimportance, and helplessness increase until they feel themselves almost disappearing. At this point in their lives they call upon their rage in its raw form to once again assert their significance, importance, and power. As a result, headlines are made.

If they had worked on synthesizing their anger in their daily lives, the big explosions would not have come. People who synthesize their anger stop acting out. They give up their power. They are willing to become weak in the presence of other people. They surrender the "cleansing" aspect of externalizing anger, they stop blaming others, and they face their own imperfections.

An example of successful synthesizing is the situation experienced by an artist in southern California. He had suffered from bouts of schizophrenia. Often he had to control his rage by leaving a situation which angered him for fear he would destroy people and things.

As is often the case with schizophrenics, he was most angry at the person he was most dependent upon—his mother. One day as she was straightening up his apartment, he felt the anger coming. In therapy he had been advised to synthesize his anger. Now, he decided, was an opportunity to try it.

The artist opened the door of his bedroom and watched his mother for a few moments. "Mom," he

began, "it upsets me when you rearrange my apartment, but I know you enjoy doing it."

The mother paused to listen, surprised by her son's
new attitude.

"I'll make a deal with you," he continued. "If you
will stay out of my bedroom and the living room, I'll
let you clean up the kitchen in my apartment and that
will be helpful."

This marked the first time the artist had ever synthesized his rage. As a result he felt in control. He
was able to influence another person's behavior so he
felt more powerful. His mother was allowed to be
useful in the young man's life but he didn't need to
destroy her to get his way. (Besides, he'd have his
kitchen cleaned!) The artist was able also to feel love.
There were no hard feelings. A potential crisis was
turned into pleasure.

A secretary was continually upset because her boss
asked her to run errands in the bank during her morning coffee break. Her annoyance became an obsession
and every day she smoldered, pouted, scowled, and
dwelled on bad thoughts. She was afraid to synthesize
her anger with healthy aggression and courtesy, so her
plight grew worse.

Encouraged by her counselor, she gained enough
assertiveness to confront her boss. She set a date and
approached his desk. This was exciting! Finally she
was going to find out what was going on and why he
always called her at coffee break.

"Myrna!" he exclaimed. "I had no idea you were
not taking your full break. It's just my schedule—I'm
plugged into calling you at 10 each morning for certain

clearances. Hereafter you take your break and I'll meet you at 10:15."

A difficult situation was resolved. Myrna synthesized her anger and now her work is a joy rather than a burden.

There are no rules for synthesizing and no guidelines to determine which aspects of ourselves to synthesize. It is usually enough to confront others and to inform them tactfully about our feelings. Sometimes we combine anger with tenderness so we hug our children extra firmly; sometimes anger is combined with eroticism so that lovers tickle each other, wrestle, and have pillow fights; sometimes anger is combined with intelligence and reasoning so that we hone our debating prowess to the sharpest intellectual powers on a given issue; sometimes we combine our anger with ambition and achieve great goals; sometimes we link anger with a sense of justice and correct injustice, helping people who are treated inhumanely, unethically, or immorally.

Unsynthesized anger nearly always has an unpleasant, antirelational consequence. But anger when synthesized can be constructive and helpful, giving its owner a sense of power without an exaggerated idea of one's own strength.

At this point in writing a phone call interrupted which provided Exhibit A for synthesizing anger.

"Dr. Sutherland, I'm going to kill my son!"

"What are you angry about?"

"I'm so angry I . . . I . . . . He spent two dollars for lunch and even loaned a dollar to a friend. I told him to spend *one* dollar for lunch. That boy . . . that . . . .

I have a kitchen knife in my hand and I'm going to stop . . . ."

"I know what your son did, but what are you angry about? What are you feeling?"

For five minutes the caller refused to understand the question. Finally she was led to do constructive things with her anger. She had experienced a loss of power and influence over her 15-year-old boy. She fantasized sitting around the fireplace cozily eating cookies and drinking milk with her son, but he found it more appealing to go to a friend's house and her dream had been crushed. In the heated argument that followed the misunderstanding the boy had screamed, "I hate you." Now the mother groaned meekly into the telephone, "Dr. Sutherland, will he ever love me again?"

"What do you feel now?"

"I feel like crying."

The woman had allowed anger to dominate her emotions rather than sitting down and having a good cry and suffering her loss of power, loss of love, loss of closeness. She was a Christian believer, so her therapist joined her in prayer as she knelt in her home and faced the truth: she did not have as much control of her son as she once had, and that was the way it should be. She could give her boy to God, and that was what she was able to do. Result: a healthier perspective, relieved emotions, strength to face a new day.

### What can we do?

What can people do if they sense they are angry but repress their anger? What can they do to get rid of their destructive tempers? What can they do if they suffer from psychologically caused aches, pain, fatigue, and tissue degeneration such as ulcers, colitis, and even cancer?

Counseling with a professionally trained, competent person is probably the most effective, but certainly not the only road, to synthesis. The following suggestions can be helpful for those who are ready to deal with their own anger.

## Pray

Prayer changes people. It has many valuable consequences. Praying about a problem is an admission that we have a problem. Praying about a problem is focusing on the fact that the solution lies within, not without. When we pray about our problems we have already taken a step away from blaming others. Praying is confessing, which causes humility. We are reminded that we are equal to others, not superior. By confessing our imperfections we recognize our need for God's gracious acceptance of us. By calling on his help we allow God to be more important in our lives. By appreciating his grace and importance we have restored fellowship (1 John 1:9). Besides this psychological aspect of prayer, by praying we also open ourselves up to divine guidance through the Holy Spirit in our lives.

## Be realistic

Infants and young children live in a world of unreality. Food, clothing, protection, and comfort all appear magically. As children, we don't have to provide these for ourselves. As a result of this magical process we develop an unrealistic fairy-tale view of ourselves. It seems to us that all of these good things happen just because we want them to happen. There is little appreciation or knowledge that others have to expend a great deal of effort to make our world so good.

Bit by bit our fairy-tale view of the world is destroyed. We go to kindergarten and get kicked by another kid just because we want to play with a toy he has. Our parents never did that.

In first grade we're handed a book and we can't make any sense out of it. We actually thought learning to read would be instantaneous. Piece by piece, our "they-all-lived-happily-ever-after world" is folded, spindled, and mutilated.

Every time reality presents to us the truth we experience anger and sadness. If we refuse to believe the truth there is more anger than sadness. If we accept the truth we experience more sadness than anger. By experiencing sadness we are saying: "I have lost a part of myself that I treasured." To a greater or lesser degree a friend of ours has died. We allow ourselves to go through the mourning process continually over a period of years and we develop a more and more realistic view of who we are and what the world is.

Through the process of mourning we find joy. Matthew 5 teaches, "Blessed are those who mourn . . . ." As we become more realistic about ourselves, our expectations in any given situation are more accurate and there are fewer disappointments. This means we can enjoy life as it *is* given to us rather than protesting because of what isn't.

As we give up our fairy-tale view of ourselves we stop expecting other people to take care of us, to do things for us, to provide our pleasure, or to be our parents.

Since we realize that people are not going to take care of us we develop an urgent desire to take care of our own needs and direct our own lives. We no longer see people as one-way objects of our own gratification but as persons with whom we can experience mutual satisfaction. Life becomes give and take rather than take and take. Love replaces demand. Other people's needs are given equality with our own.

We are neither victims of others nor masters of others. We are equals in the world, all striving the best we can to get meaning, pleasure, and fulfillment in life. Then and only then can we truly love.

### Engage in self-confrontation

To confront is to speak clearly what one sees in another. It differs from judgment in that judgment has rightness and wrongness associated with it. To judge is to say, "You are wrong or guilty." To confront is to say "This is what you did" and leave the judgment to the other person. Self-confrontation is the sometimes painful experience of admitting to ourselves what we feel. For angry persons, self-confrontation involves saying: "I am angry." "I want to hit." "I would like to kill." "I'm mad at God." "I'm mad at my wife (husband, children)." Self-confrontation is an important aspect of growth.

### Elicit confrontation by others

This is perhaps the most painful step in the process of growth. Ask people who know you to tell you their impressions. This involves great muscle strength—it involves tightening of the muscles which keep the mouth closed. Don't defend yourself *at all*. Don't try to talk them out of their impressions. Don't justify. Just listen. Recognize that they are not speaking the truth—merely their own biased impression. It is your job to sort out the truth from their own motives, needs, and fears. But if five people tell you you come across as angry, believe them.

### Accept the truth

This phase goes on regularly throughout life and can only be done in the presence of another person. It is the most emotional part of the process. We need others to help clarify our self-confrontation and to continue to accept us even though we feel unacceptable. In this phase we acknowledge the fact that we're not as powerful nor as self-sufficient, important, or perfect as we wish to be. In this phase we give up our childhood fantasies of nobility, fortune, popularity, power, beauty, strength, wealth, competence, and skill and adjust them to a realistic level.

Most people weep sometime during these mourning experiences. The question on the lips of people at this time is: "Can you accept me even though I'm not as great as I have pretended?" At this moment they need somebody there to say, "Of course!" Inevitably when we admit our weaknesses we become more lovable. We have never heard of an experience of a person being rejected at this time. Rejection comes only when you attack the other person in some way. It is our experience that in every case we are more respected and more loved when we acknowledge our unrespectable and unlovable parts. What a blessing it is to have somebody love us even when we lose our fairy-tale view of who we are.

Anger is our companion throughout life. God built it into the soul as a primary motivator for acceptance of reality, for growth, and for strength. Anger can lead to destructive behavior if not properly modified and synthesized. When synthesized, it is an important and valuable part of being human.

# Suggested Reading

Ashford, Jeffrey. *The Anger of Fear*. New York: Walker & Co., 1979.

Bellak, Leopold, et al. *Ego Function in Schizophrenics, Neurotics, and Normals*. New York: John Wiley and Sons, 1973.

Nordstrom, Carl. *Anger*. New York: Random House, 1967 (out of print).

Rubin, Theodore Isaac. *The Angry Book*. New York: Macmillan Co., 1969.

Saul, Leon Joseph, and Younger, Joan. *The Hostile Mind*. n.p., 1956.

Skoglund, Elizabeth. *To Anger with Love*. New York: Harper & Row, 1977.

Southward, Samuel. *Anger in Love*. Philadelphia: Westminster, 1973.

Stratton, George Malcolm. *Anger: Its Religious and Moral Significance*. 1923. Reprint. Darby, Pa.: Darby Books, n.d.